Write to be Published

Nicola Morgan

First edition

Proudly published in 2011 by
Snowbooks Ltd.

www.snowbooks.com

Paperback ISBN: 978-1906727-94-9
ePub ISBN: 978-1907777-51-6

A catalogue record for this book is available from the British Library.

www.writetobepublished.co.uk

Biography

Nicola Morgan was born in a boys' boarding school and has recovered remarkably well, while retaining the ability to do press-ups. After a painful struggle, she grew up to be the author of around ninety books, including category best-sellers and award-winners. She has been Chair of the Society of Authors in Scotland, an English teacher, dyslexia specialist, entrepreneur, professional cook, pillow-case repairer and trainee turkey plucker (failed). Thanks to her blog, *Help! I Need a Publisher!,* she dominates the Google rankings for the phrase Crabbit Old Bat, a fact of which she is unappealingly proud. She lives in Edinburgh and on chocolate.

Follow Nicola on Twitter as @nicolamorgan
Write to be Published – www.writetobepublished.co.uk
Nicola's blog – www.helpineedapublisher.blogspot.com
Author website – www.nicolamorgan.co.uk.

Contents

INTRODUCTION

FROM BLOG TO BOOK

I admit that it was in a mood of tetchiness that I began to blog for aspiring writers, early in 2009. I had woken one morning with an unattractive wish to harangue them for what I saw as self-defeating behaviour and frequent failure to seek out and follow the best advice available, although I knew I'd been guilty of much the same during my years before publication. When **Help! I Need a Publisher!** was born, my grumpiness somehow didn't put people off and soon the blog was being read by a large community of intelligent, hard-working writers, striving to be good enough, struggling to understand, desperate to succeed through the correct mixture of talent, perseverance, knowledge and strategy. Many were published writers already, because good writers don't stop learning, and they contribute their experiences. The comments and mutual support are a huge part of what the blog became. Many are now friends and colleagues. And when the Crabbit[1] Old Bat epithet stuck, as it quickly did, they made it difficult for me to maintain the desired atmosphere of glorious crabbitness. It was most annoying: they kept damn well agreeing with me!

A year later, with hundreds of thousands of my words and thousands more in comments by writers at all stages, it was hard for a newbie to know where to start. Hence, this book. It's not the same as the blog – it's neater, better organised, more coherent, and you can curl up with it. You can throw it at the wall when the truth hurts too much. It contains no competitions to win chocolate, no pictures of the bare feet of my fellow train passengers, no spam comments from people trying to sell me shoes. It's more polite, well-behaved, and controlled. It's still me, but it's me in a gorgeous evening dress. And stunning shoes, naturally.

WHAT THIS BOOK WILL DO – AND WHAT IT WON'T

Write To Be Published aims to show you why publishers and agents say "No". Before I was published, I'd had vast experience of this small but infuriating word: twenty-one years of it before my first novel came out in 2002. Put simply, I don't want you to take so long and WTBP is my solution, underpinned by the belief that when we understand why they say no, we can begin to make them say yes. Rejection is an occupational hazard for writers and often we have no idea

---

1   Lovely Scots word meaning grumpy and tetchy.

what we're doing wrong. My aim is to unlock the mysteries, to share with you what I wish I'd known so much earlier.

There are some things that this book can't do. I can't create something out of nothing, so I can't create talent if you have no seeds of it. I won't tell you that at the end of this road is publication, because it may not be. I won't ask whether you "have a book in you"; I assume that you do, and if you don't, you'll soon find out. We will hug no trees and utter *ommmmm* over no mysterious crystals. Being a successful writer involves working very hard. It is a butt-on-seat message.

Books on writing must choose between breadth and depth. This book puts breadth first, because breadth is what you need first, though there is also enough detail to solve many problems. Some books concentrate on a few chosen topics such as character or plot. In **Write To Be Published**, I aim to show you enough about all the important aspects of writing books for you to recognise whether you need to investigate a specific point more deeply. This book plays the role of general practitioner rather than consultant endocrinologist and we always need a general practitioner first. So, **Write To Be Published** is your first stop in your quest to discover what is wrong, or to prevent it. It may well be that this appointment with a general practitioner is all you need. If it isn't, the resources at the back will suggest further action.

You will also find a great deal of guidance on the subject of how to submit your book. Correct submission is less important than the actual writing, but it's the area where writers agonise most, and where the mistakes are easiest to avoid, so I've tried to set you straight on this.

In short, this book is for you:

* If you want to understand why publishers and agents so often say no, and thus have a better chance of making them say yes.

* If you want to discover any problems in your book and avoid them in future.

* If you are ready for hard work and prepared to have your eyes opened.

* If you simply want to write the best possible book, one which will attract readers.

* If you want to know the best ways to submit your work once you've made it wonderful.

* If you can cope with my crabbitness, irreverence and impatience.

Don't be put off by this admission of grumpiness. If you fulfil the first three criteria above, I am truly on your side. I can't wave the magic wand of publication, but I can show you some of the tricks and shed light on the sometimes confusing world of readers and writers. It is strange, but it's not as hostile or as stupid as it sometimes appears. There is method in its madness.

WHY TRUST ME?

Before believing any advice, we should always consider the credentials of the giver. There's no exam or qualification for writing this or any book and I certainly don't know everything. But my advice doesn't come just from my own experience of having around ninety books published in various genres with mainstream publishers. It also comes from contact with countless authors, agents and publishers, from both my work as Chair of the Society of Authors in Scotland and my membership of various groups and organisations. From my own work as a literary consultant and because agents often send me examples of submissions, I see for myself some of the mistakes and I learn from agents and publishers themselves why they say no. They kept telling me I should write a book. So I did.

SECTION ONE: BEFORE THE WRITING

All of you are at different stages. Some of you haven't begun a first draft and some have now completed four attempts; some are at the point of submitting a manuscript for the first time while others have been rejected already, perhaps often. Whatever stage you are at, don't consider skipping this section. The right attitude, behaviour and knowledge about how the minds of publishers[2] work, and why they make the decisions they do, are crucial to your ability to snare one of them. Yes, your book is the most important factor in your journey to publication, but your journey will be shorter and less painful if you understand the geography of the route. You can't just write a book, put fifty copies in envelopes and send

---

2   Rather than say "publishers or agents" every time, I will usually use "publishers" to mean both. If I mean one and not the other, I will specify where it is not obvious from the context. Also, I will sometimes refer to the publisher as a person, and sometimes as a company, depending on the context.

them off, expecting publishers to do anything more than fuel their wood-burning stoves with them. So, hang around: this section is essential.

MY VERY SIMPLE THEORY OF GETTING PUBLISHED

Note that I say simple. Not easy. My simple theory of getting published is this: write the right book in the right way and send it to the right publisher in the right way at the right time. If you do, it will be published.

Let's unpick that. Otherwise this will be a short book and you will not get your money's worth.

Right book – sometimes, a good writer simply hasn't written the right book. The "right book" is any book which a sensible publisher believes has enough readers and which that publisher is equipped to sell. The whole section, **The Right Book**, explains this, giving you an insight into how publishing decisions are made and how to ensure your book falls into the "right book" category.

Written in the right way – sometimes, a writer has had a good idea for a book but has not written it in the right way. There are many rules for writing, and many acceptable and unacceptable ways to break them. There are rules for genre and all manner of things for the unwary writer to stub his[3] toe on. You will need to get the structure right, develop

---

3   Or her, of course. I don't like saying "his or her" and "he or she" so I will use one or the other, haphazardly.

characters, provide narrative thrust and suspense. There are many wrong ways to write a book, even a book which sounds like the right book, and I will attempt to highlight them in the section called **Written in the Right Way**.

Sent to the right publisher or agent – you could have a brilliant idea and write it in the right way but if you send it to the wrong publisher, it will be rejected. You wouldn't believe how much time is wasted by writers sending things to publishers who don't handle that particular sort of book. No publisher handles every sort of book. Each has preferences and skills in different areas and writers need to think about this strategically. Also, there are some dud publishers you'd be wise to avoid but you can't do so unless you know what they look like. All this applies equally to agents. I will talk about this in **Submitting in the Right Way**.

In the right way and at the right time – there is no single right way, but there are very many wrong ways, and following the right advice about this will make a great difference to the speed with which you succeed. Although it is your writing and your book that will ultimately determine your success, mistakes at the submission stage can prevent a publisher from reading your book at all. And the right time? This can be hard to judge and is often where luck comes in, but there are still some ways to raise your chances and I will show you how to be canny about this. A great deal of it is about putting yourself into the shoes of the person receiving your manuscript – along with eleventy-million others – and once you know what it feels like to be in those shoes, it becomes so much easier. **Submitting in the Right Way** is where you will find all this advice about sensible submissions.

THE RIGHT TO BE PUBLISHED?

This is where I can be at my most grumpy. No, we do not have the right to be published. Neither you, nor I, nor anybody has that right. Some people spout this "everyone has the right to have their voice heard" thing, especially if the writer has suffered in some way. Well, OK, everyone has the right to speak, and everyone has the right to write. But no one has the right to expect anyone else to listen or to read it. Especially not if it's eye-bleedingly awful.

Being published is about having readers. We earn readers because of varying degrees of talent, hard work, a good idea, and knowledge about how writing works. Even then, nothing is guaranteed; good marketing and some luck also play their part. Remember an important fact about readers: they have many other pressing things to do. Being published involves trying to make lots of readers choose your book over someone else's and choose reading over all the other demands on their time.

So, we have to accept that the world does not owe any of us publication and that it will carry on spinning if our books remain unpublished. I had to learn this, too, and I took an unnecessarily long time about it. We have to be prepared to work hard, seek and welcome criticism. If you have not yet been published, it's because you have not convinced anyone that you are worth their investment. You might be, but you haven't found a way to show it. And published writers are no different: being published once is no guarantee of being published again.

If you are now spiralling into despair, be assured: if you are good enough and prepared to work, I really want you to be published. I may be crabbit but I love good books and I love good, hard-working, realistic writers. Stay with me, and I'll stay with you.

ARE RULES FOR FOOLS?

You will hear stories of writers disobeying all the rules and still getting published. Yawn, yawn, yawn. You will also hear stories of people smoking forty cigarettes a day for forty years and running across a motorway blindfolded but neither dying of cancer nor being killed by a car. This does not mean that smoking and crossing motorways blindfolded are sensible ways to behave.

Focusing on stories of successful disobedience is illogical and risky. Yes, sometimes a writer achieves a good publishing deal despite not following every rule. However, ask yourself three things:

* Do you want to raise your chances or lower them?

* Do you value your book enough to give it the best chance?

* Would you prefer to be published sooner than later?

Slavish obedience of rules is for slaves. Ignoring rules is for ignorant people. Sensible people, when offered a rule or advice, do several things: they work out whether the person offering it has reason to be trusted; they listen carefully until they understand it; they work out whether it applies to their own situation. Then they decide whether to follow, adapt or ignore it. You are sensible people. Therefore, when something I say does not seem to fit your situation, use your instinct instead. Almost any rule, once properly understood, may be broken, but you must always know why and what the effect will be.

So, no, rules are not for fools. Rules are tools and we have to learn which ones are right for each task. I will offer them to you, with an explanation if I have one, and then it's entirely up to you what you do with them. My most important rule for anything is this: apply common sense based on as much knowledge and understanding as you can acquire. And that's one you should never break.

CONFLICTING ADVICE

You will sometimes find conflicting advice for aspiring writers, whether on the internet or elsewhere. There are many good reasons for this. Publishing and writing depend to a great extent on individual passions and personal responses to books. Disillusioned writers who have turned to self-publishing[4] vent their disillusion and often misunderstand the reasons why publishers rejected them. Published authors often have

---

4   For clear and honest explanations of the various types of self-publishing and reasons to do it or not, visit How Publishing Really Works, by Jane Smith – howpublishingreallyworks.com

a narrow field of knowledge – their own experience – and may wrongly extrapolate generalisations. Some rules apply in the US and not the UK or elsewhere; some practices change over time; situations differ between genres and age-ranges. Where advice is based on expert opinion, those opinions can differ from each other. Well-meaning experts try to offer concrete answers to the specific questions you ask, when the real answer is usually, "It depends on your book." You don't like that answer, so we try to say yes or no. Sometimes the answer is yes, and sometimes it's no. Because… it depends on your book.

Sometimes advice conflicts because one side is talking rubbish. Generally, it's best to avoid taking too much notice of advice from people who have done nothing to prove that they know anything relevant. For example, an unpublished writer who has never worked in any relevant bit of publishing is not a reliable person to give you advice about how to become published, though she may give good support in other ways.

It is important, therefore, to make good judgments about whose advice you are going to take. Ask yourself how the person knows what she claims to know; whether her experience is up-to-date and specific to you. None of us knows everything about everything. US screenwriter, William Goldman, said, "Nobody knows anything." Not quite true, but it's certainly true that some know more than others and are better equipped to advise.

So, gather contacts who are likely to give good guidance. In this world of networking, with so many resources and people giving their time online, it's never been easier to find a wealth of advice and contacts, well-written articles by experts and experienced people who are often generous with their time. And when the advice of two or three or twenty-three genuine experts conflicts, just use your judgment; when experts disagree, you can only do your best to decide who to follow. Don't become rudderless: decide who to trust, and let that person be you. If you've listened enough and thought enough, you'll probably be right.

HEALTHY RESPECT

Have you already developed an unhealthy mistrust of publishers? Think they're all a load of drunken, ignorant sadists who wouldn't recognise your talent if it leapt out of a cake and showered them with promises of future wealth? This attitude will get you nowhere. If you want to be and stay published, you must learn the art of publisher-whispering. Don't shout at them in scary wannabe-style fury. They tend to hide.

What's worse, they talk to each other. A lot. They also keep moving to different companies – it's a trick they learn in publisher-school: to keep moving so authors can't catch them. What this means is that your vitriolic cursing on your blog or the unguarded email sent in anger after a glass too many of Shiraz will not only come back to haunt you: it will be the untamable poltergeist in your career, hurling precious vases at your head every time you try to approach another publisher. So, if you are feeling angry or negative about publishing or you're bruised by another rejection, don't share your feelings with anyone other than trusted friends or family. Buy a punch-bag or something. Just don't click Send.

However, it's not enough simply to hold back from retaliation. If you want to make your journey as easy as possible, you must understand and respect why they make their decisions. What may seem strange and unfair to you when you're being rejected makes much more sense when you understand it. This will help you be sanguine, and not beat yourself up every time you get a knockback.

WHY IS CRAP PUBLISHED?

Because readers like it. Because your definition of crap is not the same as the next person's. Because there are, rightly, books for everyone. You can call it eel vomit[5], as I often do, but, even if you think no one has the right to read crap, publishers have the right to publish it and readers to like it.

Of course, what we mean is: "Why was that book published and not mine, when mine is so much better?" But being published is not a competition about who can write better than someone else: it's about who can write books that capture the desires of particular categories of readers. There is no imaginary line above which you deserve to be published and below which you don't. Also, different requirements apply to different genres and readers.

---

5   My thanks to Anne Rooney, author of *10001 Horrible Facts: A Yukkopedia of Gross Truths about Everything* (Arcturus 2006) for a fascinating conversation as to which sorts of eel or hagfish vomit, but I like eel vomit.

If we want to be published, we must accept that readers are the rulers and that they want many different sorts of books and will have varying ideas about them. Often it really is a matter of personal taste. I have seen books shortlisted for awards when I think they're boring or facile; I've seen such books glowingly reviewed by people whose judgment I'd expect to be good; and I'm sure some people think my books are rubbish – indeed, they occasionally say so, usually anonymously. Yes, I do believe there are books that don't deserve to have been published. But that's life. There are people who don't deserve big salaries, or to win the lottery or be lucky or successful. But they are and we have to rise above this and focus on what we do, what we want, and what we are or aren't prepared to do to get it. Commercial success is not always the same as artistic success and we have to deal with that.

Besides, there's an art to writing good rubbish. It's not easy. Have you tried? There's a fortune to be made, I've heard.

PUBLISHERS AND AGENTS NEED TO MAKE MONEY

What, you thought they were in this as a route to heaven? Yes, they need to make money. Let's get over it.

What I mean by making money is finding enough people to buy the book in order to make a profit on the investment. What I do not mean is that money is their sole goal; or that the goal is pots and pots of money. But we should remember that they are running a business and that making a profit is a necessary aim. If you condemn them for this, you are likely to find it difficult to work with them, and they you.

Put it this way: if you were a visual artist, would you expect a gallery to take your work if the gallery didn't think it could sell it? No. So, why would you expect a publisher to do the equivalent? You have to write a book that will sell. If you can get your head properly round that concept, and work on achieving it, rather than hugging your art close to your heart where no one will see it, then your frustration may be short-lived.

NOT ALL PUBLISHERS ARE THE SAME

Some only take likely big sellers; others have an endearing passion for books and readers, and even for writers (though I prefer to leave passion out of it) and are happy to seek books they adore, even if they know there will not be large numbers of readers. Most publishers need some big sellers in order to support books that can't expect a huge market. In fact, it could be the commercial success of books you may not respect which allows your book to be published. After all, it's said that publishers make 80% of their revenue from 20% of their books.[6] As I write this – December 2010 – falling revenue from books means that publishers are finding it harder than ever to commit to niche titles because it is simply too difficult to sell enough copies. Think about it: if high discounting means that the revenue from each copy sold is lower, they must sell more copies to make the same amount

6   DTI Report: Publishing in the Knowledge Economy, 2002.

of money. This means they must work harder to sell the same titles, or pick titles which are likely to sell more copies.

The result is that, although publishers are not all the same, they would all like to sell more books, and most of them need to. If we don't consider that when we write and pitch our ideas, we do ourselves no favours.

NOT ALL AGENTS ARE THE SAME

Agents only earn a percentage of your earnings and what you earn on one book is likely to be not very much, despite substantial work by the agent, unless your success is stellar. Therefore, whereas a publisher is thinking mainly of *this* book, an agent is thinking about your career. If an agent doesn't see a reasonably profitable career in you, he may not take you on, even if your book could be published. Remember, too, that the time an agent spends on you is time he can't spend on another author and, if the other author is likely to earn him decent money, you have to ask how many low-earning authors he can afford to spend time on.

Don't expect agents or publishers to take you on if they don't think they can recoup their investment. They all need to pay the bills.

DON'T AUTHORS NEED MONEY, TOO?

Interesting question. Everyone needs money to survive, but we all have different needs and aims from our writing. Some of us want to earn as much as we can from it; for others, the motivation is the passion for writing, or the pleasure of seeing our books in the hands of readers. There's pride in being published and pride in earning something from our writing. For each of us those two things will be important in different degrees. The writer Jules Renard[7] said, "Writing is the only profession where no one considers you ridiculous if you earn no money." Sadly, many people do nowadays consider us ridiculous and sometimes we can feel ashamed of our low earnings from writing. Try to ignore them: there is no shame either in earning less because you believe in your art, or earning more because you went down the more commercial route. Make your choice and be at ease with it. But don't knock others for travelling a different route.

Some books and genres are more commercial – more likely to sell in serious numbers – than others. You need to be as realistic as possible about what sort of book yours is in terms of commercial potential. If your book is not very commercial, there is less chance of a good income for the publisher or you – though there can always be surprise best-sellers – and you must accept that this will be part of the decision to reject or accept the book.

Whatever your position on the art versus commerce continuum, when it comes to your attitude to publishers, you must temper your desire to be arty with the knowledge that everyone else in the chain – agent, publisher, bookseller – has to make enough money to keep going.

---

7   French writer, 1864-1910.

ARE PUBLISHERS EVER WRONG?

Define "wrong". You will have heard stories of famous books which were rejected many times before going on to be massive. **Lolita, Lord of the Flies, The Day of the Jackal**, and **The Wind in the Willows** are well-known examples. So, does this mean that the publishers who rejected them were wrong? You might think so, but consider some other possibilities.

Reasons why publishers might reasonably reject a book which goes on to be huge:

* It's not the sort of book they publish and therefore they would not make a good job of it. Different books require different expertise. If they'd published it, it might have bombed.

* They have filled their schedule for the foreseeable future. Publishers would be foolish to take on more than they can handle. Also, since publication is likely to be around eighteen months after the decision to acquire your book, many costs have to be paid long before they can expect income, so budgets are an important issue.

* They are scheduled to publish another book in competition with it. This *might* not be a problem but it could be – it depends on the nature of the book and the size of the publisher. It is more of a problem with non-fiction.

* Some books are unpredictably successful. The business of saying which book is going to work could never be an exact science. We can't expect publishers to throw money at everything on the off-chance.

The thought to hold onto is that when a publisher says no, he is not necessarily saying, "This is not a good book." He is saying, "This is not a book I believe I can publish well." You do not want to be published by a publisher who does not believe in your book, do you? In that case, by my twisted logic, publishers are never wrong when they reject a book.

On the other hand, they are sometimes wrong when they accept a book or at least when they pay huge money for it. There have been celebrity autobiographies which failed to live up to the expectations and investment of their publishers. And publishers sometimes over-estimate the popularity of a book, printing too many copies. These decisions can affect profits and therefore publishing strategy for long afterwards.

Most such decisions are made in good faith and with the power of successful publishing companies behind them but there are also some small, new or amateurish publishers which are not as good as others at making the right decisions, and some really don't know what they are doing when it comes to getting books into shops. I will deal with how to spot inferior publishers and agents when I talk about submitting your manuscript because part of the act of sending your book to the "right" publisher involves separating the good from the not so. I do not want you simply to be published: I want you to be successfully published.

PERFECT AUTHOR BEHAVIOUR

It may not have escaped your attention that some published authors behave unpleasantly. However, I don't recommend it, especially before publication. If your manuscript is teetering near the borderline of being accepted, you do not want to jeopardise your chances with a display of arrogance or anything else nasty.

Publishers know that published authors, being human, can misbehave and let them down. But it makes their lives easier if you don't. They do not want to have to call for assistance to scoop you out of a dodgy club at four in the morning; or to pay for counselling for the poor publicity girl you've insulted; or to find that when they send you to the Edinburgh International Book Festival you over-indulge in the Yurt[8] and become incoherent in your event.

They need you to be professional in other ways, too: to deliver your manuscript when you say you will, to write what you agreed to write, to turn up when you are supposed to, and to work with them on matters promotional. They need you to be manageable. This does not mean you have to be a doormat but it does mean you have to cultivate reasonableness and professionalism, at least outwardly.

So, in all your dealings with publishers and agents, and in your own ramblings on your blog or wherever, try to portray yourself as a person that a publisher will want to work with in a long and prosperous relationship. Be pleasant and professional. Show that you are willing to learn: attend

---

8 The famous author tent at the EIBF – I hope to see you there one day.

writing conferences and book festivals and join relevant organisations. Don't pester and don't pitch your work at inappropriate moments, such as on Twitter or when you meet an agent coming out of the toilets during a conference. Be sensitive to the glazing over of his eyes. Oh, and don't try to seduce an agent or publisher. There's no point: it's sales and marketing people who make the decision anyway and most of them are below the age of consent.

Talking about age of consent: lots of disgruntled writers, especially those of a certain age – mine – moan that they've heard you need to be sexy and young. With apologies to my colleagues, you only have to look at authors in a group to know that this is not true. I'm not saying a publisher won't love you for being camera-ready and having pearl-white teeth, but there are many ways to sell a book, and scrunched-up faces, knobbly knees and challenging body measurements are no barrier to a publishing deal if your book is good enough. They just make a difference to how you'll be promoted. If, like me, you would be little use on a catwalk and gravitation is dragging your body ungracefully gravewards, you will be able to find different selling points.

ATTITUDE TO READERS

The main reason I failed to be published for so long is that I was thinking only of myself and the gorgeousness of my prose. I thought that if I loved my words, everyone else should. Readers? Couldn't give a damn. Now I never stop thinking of the reader. Often, my readers are teenagers and they are the slipperiest creatures, their minds fizzing, desperate to go and do something more exciting. My job is to hold them, not with each chapter, or even with each paragraph, but with each sentence, each word.

It is foolish arrogance to take readers for granted. You have to know them, tune in to them, but not always give them exactly what they're expecting. You see, when I say think of them, I don't mean pander to them, but they must enjoy what you do for them, or they won't come back.

Stephen King, in his highly-recommended book, **On Writing**, talks about his "ideal reader", a person whose appreciation he is looking for, in his case his wife. This is a useful way of thinking. My own ideal reader is a distillation of all the people I hope will most appreciate the book I'm writing. Once you've had some books published, this is easier, because you learn what pleases your readership. But, somehow, at every stage, you need to develop a sense of what sort of readers you are writing for. You can't please everyone but you want to please those intended readers and you can't do that if you don't have a sense of who they are.

Ask most writers who they are writing for and they'll say, "Anyone who'll read it." Of course. But that's simplistic. It is also not easy. Writers who genuinely believe they don't think of their readers consciously must be doing it subconsciously, I argue. Perhaps thinking is not the right word: tuning in is more like it, and you can certainly tune in without thinking, once you've got the knack. The best way to understand your reader is read the same books. That way, you become an expert in what makes your reader tick, what works and what might not. Show some respect for your readers: read their books; then they might read yours.

I should add at this point that there are successful writers who say they don't think much about their readers and that they write for themselves. So, does that make my advice rubbish? I don't think so, naturally. I think it means that they happen to have instinctively tuned in to their readers without consciously thinking about it. But I come across too much unpublished and substandard self-published writing which fails to engage the reader because the writer has not begun to think about readers. And it's why I failed for so long. So, yes, write for yourself, but only if you are writing for readers, too. Readers who are like you. (As long as you're not completely odd…)

DELUSIONS OF TALENT

Whether talent is based more on nature or nurture is a fascinating but irrelevant question. By the time you're reading this book and writing your own, you either have a lot of talent or a little or anything in between. None of us can truly estimate our own talent. Actually, in order to have the determination to continue through the rejections, we probably need to believe we're better than we are, but not so much better that we blind ourselves to the need to improve. Certainly, you can expect to build on whatever you've got, through practice, following good advice, or perhaps tuition.

But, although sparks of talent can be fanned into something brighter, if there's no spark no one can light a fire.

You've seen it yourself on reality talent shows: the cringe-making hopelessness of those contestants who seem to inhabit a parallel universe. Some unpublished writers, similarly, are deluded if they think there's any point in aiming for publication. I should stress that by *deluded* I don't mean simply not being quite good enough or being rejected umpteen times: I mean being so far below the mark, so unwilling to learn, that they don't stand a hope in hell of achieving what they're aiming for. This is a harsh message, I know. If it helps, I believe that if you're reading this book and really trying to unlock the clues to good writing, you are not deluded. The ones I worry about have not even bothered to think about improving: they already think they are brilliant. They think that one day they'll win the Nobel Prize for Literature, which is not much different from me thinking I'm a dead cert for Sports Personality of the Year.

Let me tell you a story to illustrate the problem of delusions about talent. My husband and I once stayed in a rubbish hotel in the north of Scotland. The hoteliers kept advertising that they were offering quality. They thought that in order to put "locally sourced produce" on the menu, it was enough for a van from Southern Nosh[9] to arrive in full view of the guests to deliver the "local" food. Local to the south, I assume. When we pointed out that the cereal bowl was encrusted with brown stuff, they thought it was adequate to say, with a

_____
9   This was nothing like its real name. However, it was clearly based a very long way from Scotland. It also produced perfectly acceptable food. But it wasn't local.

laugh, "That'll be the toffee sauce!" They thought it was fine to provide a bed with no obvious mattress, so that every time we sat on it we jarred another vertebra. And that a lorry could reasonably recharge its freezer battery all night outside a guest bedroom and that the answer to the bleary complaint from the guests could reasonably be, "That'll be the freezer lorry."

In case you haven't got the picture yet, these deluded hoteliers believed that, whatever the shortcomings of their hotel, at least the guests would wake each morning and comfort themselves with the thought, "Praise be! There's a Corby trouser press!" Because, if you can't have decent food and a mattress and a bed big enough for two people, you can at least have a perfect crease in your trousers, ready for your walk in the hills.

This is not a pointless story. There is a treatment for this type of delusion, something those hoteliers should do in order to discover what they're doing wrong: stay in good quality places themselves. In the same way, if you wish to prevent, identify or treat any delusion about your own ability, you should read modern books in your genre and read them like a writer: analytically, honestly, greedily. Don't steal from them: admire them and aspire to them. Work out what works, and even what doesn't, and inform your own work with it.

REASONS TO BE FEARFUL

You know what they say about being careful what you wish for? Well, now that you have the right attitude to publishing, and are raring to go, I feel duty-bound to warn you about what lies ahead if you succeed. If you think published writers sit around eating chocolate, occasionally speaking a few languid words into a voice recorder, watching their assistant demi-under-publicists order another bottle of champagne or saying *mwah, dahling* to famous people, think again.

Here's why:

* You will suffer insecurity. We all do. Or most of us. And we hate the secure ones. How wouldn't we be insecure, when people tell us we're rubbish? And if anyone says nice things, they're often a) paid to, b) our parents or c) deluded (which includes our parents).

* Not only do we feel insecure, we are. Being published once means that dire sales figures can prevent book two being accepted. The secure author is incredibly rare and it certainly doesn't include me.

* People will ask you annoying questions and you won't be able to explain why your face just twisted up. If your face twists up and you don't give a smiling response, they will call you arrogant.

* The money is usually rubbish and the hours are long.

* You will go into bookshops and not find your books there. Then you will have to listen to a friend say, "I went into the bookshop in Upper Auchtermuchty and your book wasn't there. Why not?"

* Your publisher will blame you for your poor sales and

dump you. This is like being made redundant but without the money. On the other hand, writing is often like working but without the money.

✶ Your work will at some point to be reviewed negatively and this will be on the internet for ever. People will go online and spout unpleasantness. The fact that these people should be asleep instead of spewing out their dislike of your book at three in the morning, and that they can't spell, doesn't make it hurt less.

This is why we eat chocolate. It is the only antidote to insecurity that I know. Get your supplies in. And plenty of coffee and anything else that keeps you going when the going gets tough.

THE WHEELS GRIND SLOWLY

The patience fairy was otherwise engaged the day my virtues were being allocated. If I want something, I want it now; if I have an idea, I act on it now. Well, impatience is something writers must deal with. The journey from your words hitting the page to your book hitting the shops, and then to your money arriving in your bank account, is frustratingly long and slow. The ugly truth is that if the book you are working on is accepted by an agent tomorrow, you may still be two years from publication. More than that if the agent can't place it quickly, as often happens.

Here is an optimistic and very rough time-scale, starting from the moment an agent contacts you to express interest in your submission. She first asks to see the full manuscript (MS) and gets back to you a couple of weeks later, saying she loves it and she'd like to be your agent. Hooray! You meet and both agree she is the agent for you; so you sign up. She wants some improvements to the book, which might take you three months. (Or less; or more.) Once she likes your improvements, she starts to send it out. Over the next month, a couple of publishers show interest. Some negotiation goes on and a deal is struck. (This is now probably more than six months after the agent showed an interest, but could be *much* longer.) The publisher takes a couple of months to come up with a satisfactory contract, which you sign. At this point you should receive the first part of your advance – usually a third or half. Hooray again. The publication date is now set and you are unpleasantly surprised to find that it is at least twelve and perhaps eighteen months away. In other words, we could easily reach two years from first interest by an agent.

Why so long? What are you and the publisher doing during this time? The first part after the contract agreement is occupied by the editing process. Your editor probably has suggestions, which you need to deal with, if you agree. (If you don't, you need to argue about it till one of you backs down.) Once your editor is happy, the book goes to a copy-editor, who comes back to you with lots of bitty things, each of which you have to make a decision about, usually in conjunction with your editor. The same editor and copy-editor are also dealing with several other books, so none of this happens quickly. Once you are both satisfied, the text is typeset – often creating more errors for you to deal with – and then a proof-reader works on it. You check it again and finally sign it off. Meanwhile, marketing and sales departments will be using the six months prior to publication to decide on a marketing plan. (And the marketing plans of a lot of other books.) They must get it into catalogues and promotions and decide about proof copies, and some of these decisions must be made earlier than six months from publication. Large chain bookshops need to know about it and see the cover early on, for example.

This all takes time and no one would want to rush it. So, don the mask of a patient person. Do two things while you're waiting: plan your own marketing and promotion, which may well include writing a blog, planning a website and getting into networking tools such as Twitter and Facebook – of which, more in **Platforms and Profile**; and get writing the next book. Meanwhile, don't give up the day job: those royalties won't start trickling in, if at all, until at least six months after publication, and that's only if the sales are good enough to overtake your advance. You have to be in this for the long haul. But you'll be having fun and you know what they say about time passing quickly?

AND THEN THERE'S THE COMPETITION

In any one month, frighteningly many books are published. Many people think there are far too many. Every year in the UK, around 120,000 titles are published – not including the self-published ones – though that number is somewhat skewed by such things as maps and reissues of Chaucer or whatever. The online book store, The Book Depository, has around three million titles and each new book competes with those for attention. Very scary. It's also worth remembering that published writers have to face identical facts. But forewarned is forearmed and I am about to warn you a bit more.

It's not just the scale of the competition that we need to worry about: it's the small number of books people buy. It's not easy to find reliable UK figures for this, but I've seen surveys that suggest that UK readers buy on average six books a year. They may *read* more than that but it's the buying that we're bothered about here. The Guardian newspaper[10] reported frightening figures from the US, including the finding that 25% of Americans had read no books in the past year, and that even discounting all those non-readers, readers read on average seven books. Factor in the fact that a reader won't make his limited choice from any books, but from books that fit his existing reading tastes. Factor in gender and age differences, which can affect our choices.

Now remember those 120,000 new UK books every year. And factor in the books published last year, and the thousands still in print from previous years, decades, generations, centuries. And the fact that according to Google, there are – or were in July 2010 – almost 130 million separate titles, in other words 130 million separate options from which readers could choose. Finally, factor in the fact that the vast majority of new books are not debut books, as you hope yours will be.

Take a deep breath. Now tell me why you think that your work in progress is so compelling that a total stranger should pick it to be one of the few books he chooses to read in a year? Not only pick it but invest money and time, precious time, engaging with the words you happen to think are worth reading. Now do you understand why it is and will always be so difficult to get a publishing deal?

---

10   guardian.co.uk/books/2007/aug/22/news

Still here? I have one last tactic to deter you.

DEALING WITH TAXI-DRIVERS

If you become published, you will one day have an incredibly annoying conversation with a taxi-driver. I have no advice for these situations, as I don't condone physical violence. Here's one that happened to me earlier:

TD: So, what's your line of business?

NM: I write books.

TD: Really?

NM: Yes.

(I am expecting the regular, "They say everyone's got a book in them." To which my answer would be either, "If so, that's usually where it should stay," or, "Yes, but would anyone want to read it?" Unfortunately, this particular story goes beyond such ordinariness.)

TD: So, how do you get a book published then?

NM *(takes a deep breath, wondering where to begin)*: Um…

TD: Because anyone can write a book, can't they? *(Silence.)* Not meaning to be insulting or anything, but anyone can. I've got a friend who's writing one. He says it's easy. Unless you're dyslexic or something.

NM: Actually, you could be a great writer and still be dyslexic.

TD: Well, that proves it – anyone can write a book. If they've got time. Like, I've often thought of writing a book but I've never had time.

NM *(tempted to ask, "What about when you're waiting at*

a traffic light? Or your passenger has just decided she'd rather walk?"): Actually, it's extremely difficult. We may make it look easy, but you've no idea of the incredibly difficult technical skills and spectacularly creative gifts that are involved.

TD: Well, I suppose you'd start by writing a children's book. Like, one of those ones with just a few words and mostly pictures. That must be really easy – most of the work is done by the artist, isn't it?

NM *(wondering how much it would hurt if she flung open the door and threw herself out)*: Trust me, it's very difficult indeed. Otherwise, why do so many people try to get published for years and years?

TD *(on transmit and not receive)*: Mind you, you'd be rich, wouldn't you? They earn a fortune, some of these children's authors. You read about it all the time.

NM *(wondering why she didn't put a handy weapon in her bag before coming out)*: You don't want to believe everything you read in the papers.

TD: I don't have much time for books. Like my son – but that's boys, isn't it? Got more important things to do. My daughter now, she's a really great reader. She read the whole of the last Harry Potter book in about ten days.

NM *(having lost will to live)*: Really? How old is she?

TD: Twenty-five. My wife and I, we always told her she could be a writer. Thing is, she doesn't have time. But they say everyone's got a book in them, don't they?

The journey ended at this point, the taxi-driver getting no tip and me stomping to my front door prior to off-loading onto my long-suffering husband who had many times in previous years wondered when the psychotherapy was going to work.

Now, pick yourself up, have a cup of coffee and then come back because we are now going to put into practice that simple theory of getting published: write the right book in the right way, and send it to the right publisher in the right way, at the right time.

SECTION TWO: THE RIGHT BOOK

WHAT DO PUBLISHERS WANT?

The simple but unhelpful answer is that they want a great book, which lots of book-buyers will want to read, and which they will talk about to their friends. This is like the Holy Grail: desirable, elusive, unpredictable, and you don't know what it is until you see it. On the other hand, it is not like the Holy Grail, because "what publishers want" could come in many guises, in thousands of books that haven't been written.

No publisher is only looking for one thing; and they will often be looking for different things from each other. Ask them what they want and you will hear answers along the lines of, "something that really grips me", "superb writing", or, "a fresh voice, something different, but, um, not too different". For you, this feels too vague and unhelpful. It is, however, worth bearing in mind because it does highlight the subjective aspects of acceptance. And rejection.

But publishers must also apply as much objectivity as

possible. As I've mentioned, commercial reality means that they need to make money, at least enough to cover costs and return something to their shareholders. So, when they make their decisions, they are working out – using their understanding of their own company, along with gut instinct – whether your book is likely to sell if they take it on. They are combining subjectivity with objectivity. And two publishers might easily reach two different conclusions and yet both be right – for them.

Here are some other answers to the question, "What do publishers want?"

THEY JUST WANT SOMETHING TO LOVE

Whoever takes your book must love it. I mean *love*. Not just think it's fairly goodish and sort of OK. Not even just know that it is decently written and follows the rules of its genre. The editor will have to argue for your book in front of a meeting of sales and marketing people – see **The Decision Process for Publishers** – people who haven't read it and may never read it, and to persuade accountanty people to allocate a budget for it. So the editor has to be damn sure, and is not allowed to get it wrong too many times.

The editor has to make a judgment about what other people are going to love, or can be persuaded to love, and that's not easy if he doesn't feel strongly about the book himself. So, what an editor is looking for is a book that bowls him over.

Or else a book which so beautifully fits the zeitgeist and/or the conventions of a particular genre that he can feel confident about taking it to that meeting and arguing passionately that it is perfect for this publisher.

Sometimes, with writing which is designed to fit a strict and specific formula, I'll grant that the editor may not have to love it, but he must still be 100% convinced that it fits the formula. Examples would be a book that forms part of an existing series or one that has specific guidelines such as those published by Mills & Boon.

Discovering that you've written a book which publishers like but don't love is one of the most frustrating things about trying to become published. I spent quite a long time in that position. This book aims to show you some ways of breaking that barrier and finding the elusive ways of writing a better or more publishable book.

BUT NOT JANE AUSTEN

The Jane Austen Delusion is the name I give to a perennial story that you'll come across in even the more intelligent news reporting. It goes like this.

IGNORANT PUBLISHERS FAIL TO RECOGNISE JANE AUSTEN

Aspiring writer, Major "Ig" Noramus, 49, caused red faces in the offices of global publisher, Dreams Unlimited, when he submitted the first chapter of Jane Austen's novel, Persuasion, disguised as a sample of his own work. When Dreams Unlimited's senior editor, Frank Lee Wright, rejected Noramus's work as being "not right for us" and added the comment that it was "unlikely to achieve critical acclaim", the Major was shocked that the editor was unable to recognise a work of proven genius. Ig Noramus says he is now going to self-publish his novel, a sci-fi-rom-com with elements of fantasy and horror, "because that way I can bring my talent to readers, by-passing the broken model that is traditional publishing."

Major Ig Noramus has failed to understand certain things:

* Jane Austen is not what publishers are looking for. They are looking for a book that has not been written before.

* Each publisher focuses on certain sorts of books and it is up to each to choose which books to publish.

* If a hitherto unseen Jane Austen title were discovered and published today, it would be published because JA wrote it and that would be why it would sell; if you wrote a book that was exactly like a book JA might have written, you would simply have been imitating JA, and since you are not JA you are of absolutely no interest whatsoever. It is logically possible that a modern market might exist for books written in JA's precise style, but any publisher is at liberty to choose not to publish JA imitations.

* The reason that the publisher rejected it was not a failure to recognise the talent of JA. The actual reason for rejection was the decision that the style and subject-matter was not

likely to sell in today's market. The Major proved nothing but his own name.

* It's entirely possible that the publisher did recognize JA's work but couldn't be bothered to tell the Major how riotously amusing he was.

SAME BUT DIFFERENT

Publishers want something that is sufficiently the same and yet sufficiently different. If the same, it must not be too the same, unless it's supposed to fit a formula. If different, it must not be so different that people are confused or that their expectations are missed. Some publishers will take a risk with something experimental – though less so in difficult financial times – but most can't, because it will be too hard to sell, unless a virtue can be made of its difference. It's not easy to sell a book by saying to people, "You know how you normally read that sort of book? Well, this is *not* like that but we still want you to buy it."

This is where it comes down to knowing your genre and your readers. If you haven't read the most recent books within your genre, you simply won't know if your book is too similar to another or too avant-garde for the readers. In other words, you won't know whether it's a good fit. If you know your genre – and therefore its readers – you will be able to achieve the correct amount of sameness and difference. Otherwise you will be aiming for a target you can't see.

In non-fiction, the need for difference is crucial, more so than for sameness, as long as the book does have an obvious place to sit on the shelf. For example, suppose you are writing a book about surviving cancer. There are many books that tackle this subject, so there will be an easy place to shelve and find your book; there are also many potential readers for it. But your book needs its special difference, its unique selling point, otherwise it won't stand out amongst the competition. Without that difference, it is unlikely to be taken by a publisher.

BAND-WAGONS AND TRENDS?

The two things are not quite the same, but we can consider them together. A band-wagon is more specific than a trend; it also has both the potential to generate many sales and the potential to be highly transient. Vampires in books are an example of a band-wagon. A trend is vaguer, broader. Examples of trends might be "increasing violence in crime fiction" or "the appearance of older women in romantic fiction". (That isn't an actual trend as far as I know, but a girl can dream.)

Trying to jump onto a band-wagon is a waste of time, for one reason: even if your current work in progress were accepted as soon as you'd finished it, it wouldn't hit the shops for well over a year after that, by which time your band-wagon will have vanished in a cloud of dust.

As for trends, there's more point in trying to join them, but it's still not easy and is only necessary to an extent, and more in some genres than others. You don't want to hit a trend that's on its way out or that has evolved into something different – and, because of the time-scale I mentioned above, this is quite possible. On the other hand, many trends hang around for ages and, if they've been successful, don't entirely disappear. So, do keep up with what's happening in publishing – there are some suggested resources at the back of this book – and try to judge which trends are sufficiently robust to follow.

What about predicting the next band-wagon or new trend? If you find anyone with that particular crystal ball, please tell me. To be honest, however, I really wouldn't bother thinking about it. Just write a great story. That's one trend that won't go away.

In non-fiction the situation is a little different. Trends and band-wagons tend to be highly topical and therefore your main risk is that by the time your book is finished it's not topical any more. Some publishers can bring out a non-fiction title extremely quickly, and they usually know who they want to write it. The hitherto unpublished writer has to move very quickly and cannily. Also, whereas you could have any number of novels inspired by a particular topic, the number of non-fiction titles that the market can sustain on that subject is likely to be smaller. You will need to find a special angle for your book.

So, while it's worth being aware of trends and band-wagons, and more so for non-fiction, it's not worth getting in a twist about them. That's why people will tend to say, "Write what you want to write. Write from the heart." That's what I say, too, but with certain provisos, depending on how keen you are to be commercially successful, because the thing about hearts is that they tend to make emotional, rather than clever, decisions. Yes, write from the heart, but engage your head, too.

WHAT IF SOMEONE GETS THERE FIRST?

One of the heart-stopping moments in any writer's life is hearing that another author is about to produce a book which sounds horribly similar to the one we are writing. Our instinct is to believe that this is The End, and that we must now ditch the fabulous idea.

Calm down. It happens and it doesn't usually matter, because your book *will* be different. Certainly, it is worth making every effort to ensure that your story will be as different as possible. Certainly, too, you would want to clarify the difference when submitting the idea, and you certainly wouldn't approach the same publisher. This is especially true for non-fiction.

But often, and particularly for fiction, these things matter less than you would think. I have a true story to illustrate this.

THE EXTRAORDINARY COINCIDENCE

In October 2001, my first novel, **Mondays are Red**, was published. I'd been writing it during 2000. Being unpublished, and not knowing any published authors, let alone a famous one, I had no way of knowing what any other author was writing in his own garret.

Mondays are Red is a teenage novel about a 14 year-old boy called Luke who has synaesthesia.

A month later, award-winning Tim Bowler's umpteenth novel, **Starseeker**, was published. He would also have been writing it during 2000, while I was writing mine. Neither of us could have known this.

Starseeker is a teenage novel about a 14-year-old boy called Luke who has synaesthesia.

Because they were published in consecutive months, we had some joint reviews. (Lucky me, a debut author being reviewed and interviewed alongside a successful one.) But no one accused either of us of plagiarism, because it obviously wasn't. It couldn't have been, time-wise, and, despite the identical descriptions above, they are two utterly different stories.

Consider the following: if **Starseeker** had come out while I was still writing mine, I'd have changed the name and probably the age of the protagonist because the last thing I'd want is to appear to plagiarise – and I'd have panicked, horribly; I might even have cried.

Tim Bowler and I became friends and discovered we thought alike in many ways. "That's not very interesting," I hear you say. No, but there's something else. When we became friends, I was writing another book, which had the provisional title of **Apocalypse**. Luckily, authory friends tend to tell each other what they're writing. "What you writing at the moment?" I asked.

"It's called **Apocalypse**," he replied. And since his

Apocalypse was coming out before mine, guess who decided to change her title, even though there's no copyright on titles? Mine became **The Passionflower Massacre**.

So, the fact that your concept sounds like an existing book says nothing about whether the story is going to be the same. It's most unlikely to be the same in any important way. Clearly, however, it is theoretically possible that your idea might be too similar to something else. In which case, you may need to go to a very large forest, stand in the middle of it and scream loudly. You would even be forgiven for stamping your feet.

It's also true that a publisher won't want a book which is similar to one it already has or is about to publish. You can't be expected to know what any publisher is about to publish, so this will be bad luck on your part if you send yours to the same place.

So, if you discover that something terribly similar has been done or is about to come out, my advice is to stay calm, think about whether your idea could be altered to have a different slant, and perhaps wait a while. Your idea could have its day later and in a different, perhaps better form. But before that, consider that the other book might not be half as similar as you fear.

DOES SIZE MATTER?

"How long should my book be?" This seems like a minor issue, and indeed it is, but it is a question that writers often ask. Very often, the answer you will get is, "A book should be as long as it should be." That's an eyeball-rolling, pencil-snapping answer if ever I heard one. Certainly, a book's length must feel right for that book. As a reader, you know what it's like when a book feels too long or when an ending comes so quickly that you sense that the writer had a burning deadline painfully close to her posterior.

Are there any rules about length? There are certainly some conventions that look like rules, though they are the sort of rules that are ripe for breaking, as the later Harry Potter books show. (On the other hand, you should not use exceptions to prove rules and nothing that extraordinarily successful authors have done should be taken as proof of anything except extraordinariness.) As a debut author, you take a major risk if you break rules of length too obviously. Further than saying that and frowning at you slightly from over my spectacles, I will give you no firm rules.

But I do have some guidelines:

* For children's books, it's important to adhere to the length of normal books for the *specific* age-range. "Specific" because the average length for books for 5-7s is not the same as that for 7-9s. I won't list suggested averages for every age-band, because it's not just about the age of the reader but the type of book and its purpose. So, all you can do is decide what existing modern books yours is *most like* and do some sample word counts. Keep within 10% of what you discover. And that's a guideline only.

* For a debut author, it is more important to keep within norms than it is for established authors.

* There tends to be more variation within literary fiction

than within a genre; and each genre will have different norms. (A good reason for knowing how your own genre works.)

* In non-fiction, it's more open, but shorter is generally better than longer, for commercial and cost-based reasons. Simply, a long book will cost more to produce and have a higher price-point; a more expensive book is usually harder to sell than one at a lower price-point. You'd need to be a very well known expert or have an extra compelling idea to get away with an over-long book.

* If a book is too short, a reader may decide that it's "not worth it" – yes, we all know that length not does equal quality but readers often think in terms of value being relative to the amount of time the pleasure may last. It's not entirely a foolish point, actually, though neither is it sufficient.

* If a book is too long, there are two risks: it may put *some* readers off, particularly in the case of children's/YA books; and it will be more expensive to produce, because more pages cost more money and a heavier book incurs more warehousing, packaging and delivery costs.

* A good target for a commercial adult novel, such as a romance or an historical novel, is 100,000 words. I have heard publishers ask for that as a minimum, though I've heard others refuse to give such a firm rule. If you head way over the 150,000 mark, you could be straying into "too long" territory, but it *really does depend*. Know your market.

* Some genres suit a longer word count: fantasy and sagas, for example.

* A novella – something under, say, 45,000, and aimed at adults – is unlikely to be published as a first novel. It's a simple commercial reality: readers are unlikely to buy something so short by an unknown author when the price they'll pay is likely to be the same as for a longer novel. However, this could all change with the rise of e-publishing, where length is less obvious.

* Whatever the word count of your first draft, losing some words would almost certainly benefit it because your writing will be tighter.

* If you have to make your novel longer, don't do this simply by padding it with more words. You should add new elements entirely, such as new scenes or a plot strand. If you just pad it, you will make it drag. (There are some tips about this in **Editing Essentials**.)

HOOKS

A hook is a way of describing your book in a concise and enticing way. It is crucial to your ability to catch a publishing deal. Between agent and customer, many people must be hooked. The agent must hook an editor, who must persuade the other decision-makers in the company – usually the sales and marketing people; the sales team will hook the booksellers and reviewers, who will hook potential customers. At every point, each has only a very few seconds in which to snare the listener.

There's another reason why you need to be able to describe your hook quickly and fluently: every now and then, someone will ask, usually without warning, "So, what's this book you're writing, then?" If it's a friend, you can get away with a creative air of secrecy, tapping the side of your nose and claiming that an artiste cannot reveal anything at such a delicate stage. But imagine that you've bumped into Mr Hot-Shot Agent and he asks you what your book is about. It's not much good if you blush and stutter, "Well, it's kind of um, difficult to explain, but it's sort of about a man and a woman and they, well, fall in love, but it's much more interesting than it sounds…" Watch your potential publishing deal float out of the window.

Good hooks make the listener think, "Wow! I must have that book!" They perform the same function as the blurb on the back cover, but are ideally even shorter. In fact, the best way to think of it is to imagine that you're writing the blurb for the back cover but that you need to halve the length. Spend time honing your hook to its essence, so that you can say it in fewer than ten seconds. Your listener might then ask a question; this means you probably did a good job and you're allowed to expand a little. If Mr Hot-Shot Agent's eyes glaze over, you need to worry. Do learn to detect the early signs of glazing over.

In practice – and you certainly should practise – you will sometimes have more and sometimes less time in which to explain your book. So you really need several versions of the hook, from the eight word one to something like a couple of lines. The shortest one is sometimes called a strap-line: those few words printed beneath the title and never longer than half a line. It gives the potential reader an intense flavour of the book and it really must zing.

It's never too early to think about your hook. I usually work on mine before I've even begun to write the book. This has two benefits: it helps me focus on the essence of my book while I'm writing it. And it will roll off my tongue when I am suddenly asked to pitch it. Later on, you will need your hook on many occasions. You will learn which versions work best as you gauge reactions. You may even begin to bore yourself with it. This is a good sign, because then you will probably make it even shorter.

HIGH-CONCEPT BOOKS

A high-concept book is, essentially, one with an extra-strong hook. It is easy to sell because the idea has wow factor and is easy to explain *very* quickly. The wow factor often comes from a sense of, "Why didn't I think of that? That's going to sell in shedloads."

Sometimes, in a high-concept book, the premise will sound unbelievable, which is part of the sit-up-and-notice factor. **Snakes on a Plane** is a film with a high-concept idea – you feel drawn to see it just to discover how such a wacky idea could be a film. In a high-concept book the stakes are often extra high, at least for the main character(s) if not for the whole world. Your main character needing to lose weight in time to fit into a holiday bikini is *not* high stakes. The end of the world being nigh, or a man needing to save his son's life, are very high stakes, for the world and for the man and his son respectively.

Below are some books which might be classed as high-concept. In each case, the essence is easy to explain briefly; there is a sit-up-and-notice factor and there are high stakes; and each was very successful in terms of both critical acclaim and sales. (Note, however, that you often have high-concept without critical acclaim. High-concept is about commercial potential; literary merit is secondary and inessential.)

The Life of Pi by Yann Martel – boy ship-wrecked on powerless boat with dying zebra, hyena and tiger called Richard Parker.

The Curious Incident of the Dog in the Night-Time by Mark Haddon – an autistic savant with a fear of yellow finds a dead dog and sets out to solve its killing.

The Road by Cormac MacCarthy – a man will do anything to avoid having to kill his young son, as they flee across America in the horrifying aftermath of global warming.

Jurassic Park by Michael Crichton – a theme park uses the DNA of dinosaurs and brings them to life, with terrifying and chaotic consequences.

Do note, however, that your book does not *have to be* high-concept in order to be taken by a publisher, so don't go hunting high-concept at the expense of good writing. In fact, if every book were high-concept, reading would become a nightmare of over-excitement. It's just that if you happen to come up with such an idea, it may very well fit the "what publishers want" category.

THE DECISION PROCESS FOR PUBLISHERS

In the old days, the publisher's acquisition process was simple. An editor, male, wearing a tweed jacket and brown suede shoes and taking an old-fashioned attitude to personal hygiene, would read your manuscript over a glass of port at his club, be bowled over by the beauteousness of your piercing insight into the life-cycle of the Lesser Galapagian monkfish, finish his dinner at the Athenaeum, totter to bed, totter out of it, make a quick phone-call to the office and tell them that he'd acquired a book and that he'd tootle along to tell them all about it once he'd finished a long lunch with his new best friend, you, the author. If a marketing department existed, which it probably didn't, the editor would never have met anyone in it, and if he did, he wouldn't talk to them because he was far more important than them.

Lest that paints an unfairly negative view of the old days, let me also point out that very often, especially in the more recent old days, the process involved a passionate, inspirational and knowledgeable editor falling dippily in love with your book and being allowed to make the decision over a long lunch, often to the benefit of all concerned.

Occasionally, but decreasingly so, that still happens. But most publishing companies, large or small, now follow the process below (or something similar), and you would do well to understand it. Publishing was always a business, and businesses have always focused on making profit, but business has changed and models and methods are different. There have been two main changes in publishing in recent years. First, the removal in 1997 of the UK price control for books means that books now compete, often suicidally, on price. Second, editors are lower down the hierarchy than before. Sales and marketing departments make the decisions, even if editors are the ones who find and fall in love with books, and hone them to perfection. But sales and marketing are essential cogs in the wheel and authors must understand their needs, too. Since this book aims to reveal why publishers so often say no, I'm now going to show you how the decisions are usually made.

Note: if a publishing company nowadays does not follow a similar procedure to the one I am about to describe, ask them what makes them so much wiser than everyone else. If they insist that they don't need to think about such unpleasant things as projected sales figures or marketing strategies, do a bit of investigation to find out what sort of coverage their last few books got. It's hard to discover sales figures unless you have access to Nielsen BookScan, but some searching for reviews, evidence of support and availability of the books in actual bookshops will go a long way to showing you whether this publisher has a clue about selling books. Because, please note, it's the publisher who is supposed to market and sell the books – although authors nowadays do a great deal to help, it is the publisher's job.

Obviously, a very small company won't have as many staff as a larger one and the system of acquiring a book may have fewer stages and be less complicated than the example below, but the thought processes should be the same. As long as they are thinking about all these things, it doesn't matter whether discussions are held in a shiny boardroom or a local coffee shop.

THE FIRST STEPS

First, the editor must believe strongly that this is the right book for this publishing company and that he will be able to persuade marketing and sales departments that it will be easily marketed and sold.

Second, depending on the size of the company and the seniority of the editor, he might pass the manuscript or proposal to another editor for a second opinion. There is usually a regular editorial meeting at which editors' hunches about various books are discussed.

Third, after getting your book through the editorial meeting, the editor works out an acquisitions proposal and begins to sweat in preparation for the acquisitions meeting. At that meeting, he will need to justify his love of your book to the hard-nosed, pointy-lapelled, French-polished people in sales and marketing who have diplomas and keep going on unnecessary assertiveness courses.

THE ACQUISITIONS MEETING

At this meeting, the editor and all the sales and marketing people must decide the answers to certain questions – or most of them, as some can only be provisional. Remember, importantly and frighteningly, that the people in sales and marketing have not read your book – the most they'll see is a synopsis and small sample, but often not even that. On this basis, and with the editor fighting for your book, they must all decide:

* Is this book right for this company? Where will it fit on the list? Will this be a "highlight" title or lower down the pecking order?

* Will it be easy to sell? Will the big book chains like it? Who is the readership? Gap in market? Hook? Unique selling point? Proposed timing of publication?

* The author – who? Publishing history? (If you've been published before, this can help but not if your publishing history is marred by bad sales. If it is, the publisher will need to work out if those sales were simply through bad luck or bad marketing, and perhaps decide to ignore them because this new book is quite different.) Marketable life-story? (Not essential, but it helps if you have one. But "Penniless single mother writing wizard fantasy series in café with small daughter in buggy because can't afford heating bills" has been done ...) Does the author have an existing platform? Is he likely to work well at promotion? I'll say more about this in the section called **Platforms and Profile**.

* Finance – budget: what advance will be necessary? When might this be recouped, based on projected sales figures? What will be the price-point for the book? Cost of production, based on page count, format and any illustrations and expected print-run. Necessary marketing spend?

In short, they must decide whether they can spend

thousands of pounds, knowing that they won't get anything back for perhaps two years.

When they say yes, they are taking a gamble. It's an informed one but it's a gamble nevertheless. If they lose, they lose money but they also lose whatever book they could have taken if they didn't take this one, because they can't take all the good books that cross their desks. They are also taking a punt on you, the author, and hoping that you will be as good for them as they will be for you, and that there's every chance of a long career for you with them, unless this is a celebrity memoir we're talking about, in which case all common sense evaporates and gibbering lunacy takes centre-stage.

You can now see why the process is rarely quick, unless your book is absolute rubbish, in which case it can be horribly quick, because you won't reach the editorial or subsequent meetings. (But a delay is not always good news. It's far more likely that no one's read it yet.)

On the one hand, this is all too horrible to think about for you. It is painful to think of your dreams being deconstructed by strangers. On the other hand, you do not get as far as the acquisitions meeting if you don't have what it takes. So, take it as a very hopeful sign, even if the answer on this occasion is not the one you desperately want.

RIGHT FOR THE GENRE

WHO CARES ABOUT GENRE?

You might be thinking, "But I've written a great story. Why does it have to fit a particular genre? Why can't I be original?" Thing is, booksellers want to know where to put your book and who to recommend it to. They need to know this because readers usually like to know what they're about to spend money and hours on. Booksellers don't have time to explain every book in detail and readers don't have time to make over-complicated judgments about what a book might be like, when they have vast numbers to choose from. Readers tend to make fairly quick decisions based on a few criteria involving their personal preferences, and one of those is usually genre.

Of course, genres often overlap and blur, and contain many shades. That's right and proper. However, one reason why a publisher might reject a book is that it feels as though it falls too painfully between two stools, and that booksellers will therefore find it hard to shelve and sell. So, do think carefully about which pigeon-hole your book will peep from. Even if it incorporates two genres, it should have one main genre and I advise you to focus on that in the main thrust of your story and also in your submission. Only if your book is both startlingly original and eminently sellable can you avoid this.

BIG PIGEON-HOLES AND LITTLE ONES

A big pigeon-hole is the genre – such as travel writing – and it is one of the first things you have to tell a prospective agent or editor. But there is more to it than this. You should also be aware of the small pigeon-hole – the more specific group of books within which yours sits. For example, within travel writing there are different types: ones that relate a new life in one place, such as **A Year in Provence** by Peter Mayle; or which relate a specific journey, such as **The Man Who Cycled The World** by Mark Beaumont; or straightforward travel guides. Within historical fiction there are many different types: extremes of literary or commercial and everything between; light, social, grim or martial; historical romance or historical detective fiction; alternative[11] history; books in the style of Bernard Cornwell, Pat Barker or Tracy Chevalier. In the crime genre, the readers of Peter James, Ian Rankin, Kate Atkinson and Aline Templeton have quite different expectations from each other. So, you need to know more precisely where your book sits than simply that it is travel writing, historical fiction or crime.

THE RULES OF THE ROOST

Different genres and sub-genres have different requirements. Each one also changes over the years, so what was required or desired ten years ago will be different now, and will not generally reverse as other types of fashion do. New genres

---

11   Alternative or alternate history: where the author takes a period and
changes something substantial, imagining for example, that Queen Victoria was
assassinated.

or combinations of genre *can* be created, but if you are too avant-garde or try a combination which has not been done before, you risk rejection, simply because there will be no pigeon-hole for it.

I am more rule-breaker than rule-follower by nature but I believe that we can only pointfully break a rule if we know what it is and why it's there, and that includes the rules and conventions of genre. I'm not saying you have to follow them slavishly: I am saying know them, and know your readers, and then you will know what rules you can break and why; and the risks.

KNOW YOUR FELLOW-PIGEONS – WHY YOU MUST READ IN GENRE

The only way to understand the above in relation to your genre is to know the other pigeons lodging with you. In other words, read the books which are similar to yours. (I knew I would become boring on that point.) Then you can write a novel which fits perfectly within an existing sub-genre and yet make it stand out by being sufficiently different: not so different that it is rejected by its fellow pigeons and pigeon-fanciers, but different enough that it earns their respect.

(No more stretching the pigeon-hole metaphor. It long ago reached the point at which stylists will have been pecking their feathers.)

Here are the risks you run by not keeping up-to-date with what's being written *currently* in your chosen genre.

* The Enid Blyton Trap. There are countless aspiring writers out there who have decided they fancy writing a

children's book because they remember enjoying them so much when they were little. Well, with all respect to Ms Blyton, the world has changed. We don't have lashings of ginger beer any more but we do have health and safety and mobile phones. So, if you don't read the modern stuff, you risk looking like some patriarchal buffoon who hasn't noticed that the Empire has fallen and there's quail's egg on his cravat.

* Not knowing what's already been done. You might not realise that a topic, voice or character has already been done to death or has recently been tackled in a high-profile book. You could look very ignorant.

* Not having commitment to a career in this genre. Thing is, one book is not enough. Your agent or publisher needs to build a career with you and you must feel comfortable with the genre if you are to write several books in it.

* Showing ignorance in your covering letter. Faux pas based on ignorance of genre are common in these letters.

* Remaining outside the world of your future fellow authors. Real writers read. I spend a lot of time with other writers in my field and I would know if one of us wasn't up-to-date with reading. You don't have to read everything, but I'd have a very low opinion of someone who couldn't join us in our own passion and yet who presumed to reap money from it.

* Arrogance. You might not feel arrogant, but it's what a potential agent will think if you show that you don't read in the genre. It displays a sense of, "Yeah, well, it's easy to

do what these crime fic/YA/pic book authors do – I can do that, easy as falling off a bike." You can do yourself a nasty injury falling off a bike.

Within the space of this book, I could not cover each genre separately. Whether you write non-fiction or fiction, crime, romance, literary fiction or short stories, I recommend that you look for groups, books, blogs, and online resources to help inform you further – and I list some at the end of this book. My blog[12] also contains posts on each of the main genres, with comments and quotes from writers in those areas and resources that they recommend. This is one of the ways in which networking can really help you: listen to other people in your field. Many published writers blog and are generous with advice.

LITERARY FICTION

"That's not a genre, you silly woman," I hear you say. Fine: technically speaking, there's commercial or genre fiction and, separately, there's literary fiction. But literary fiction is still a category, another pigeon-hole.

The thing about literary fiction that makes it different from other genres is that breaking rules is almost expected. But you must still know those rules; it's the difference between me stuffing a dead animal and Damien Hirst stuffing a dead animal: obvious to the experts. (I believe.) Literary fiction

---

12   In case you've forgotten, Help! I Need a Publisher! – helpineedapublisher. blogspot.com

is, in theory, like lacrosse: it has no boundaries. However, as with lacrosse, you can't simply run away with the ball. Whistles blow and people shout at you. Messing around too much sometimes alienates people – readers as well as the gatekeepers such as publishers – so it's a risk. But risk is part of the nature of literary fiction.

On the other hand, although it is traditionally untraditional, literary fiction does not have to break the mould every time. It might have a traditional structure, for example, and yet be marked by style or voice. One could say that it focuses more on form and language than on plot or character, though writers should not forget that for most readers plot and character are what keep them reading. Although pageturnability and narrative thrust are more noticeably essential in commercial fiction, there are few readers of any sort who can read something with no oomph in it at all.

If literary fiction is your aim, prepare for some uncomfortable truths:

* It is harder to publish. Much harder.

* And fewer people read it. (That's why it's harder to publish.) So, even if you are published, you are unlikely to be able to give up the day job yet.

* The merit of a literary manuscript is harder to judge, because it's less about ticking the boxes, so personal taste is more a factor. That's another reason why it can take longer to find a publisher to love it confidently enough to publish.

Literary fiction *can* sometimes succeed commercially, though. Such success usually relies on winning or being shortlisted for one of the big literary prizes, something which is notoriously difficult to predict. Many very good books narrowly miss these lists and end up selling significantly fewer copies than those which narrowly make the shortlists.

It's also important to add that each of the other genres has its more "literary" end and more "commercial" end. I ask you not to sneer at one or the other: simply recognise where your book will sit, and work within or adapt the rules accordingly.

COMMERCIAL FICTION

Commercial fiction generally means fiction which fits a specific genre and which is not literary fiction. It may be called genre fiction. It is characterised by page-turning quality and narrative thrust, often focusing on plot and character more than language. A commercial novelist expects to sell more copies than a literary one, whereas a literary one hopes to be reviewed in serious places. Of course, there's an overlap. And of course everyone would like to sell lots of books *and* have reviews everywhere but this is about expectations and priorities.

Some novels turn out to be commercially successful despite not fitting a specific genre. This is sometimes called general fiction. An example would be **The Curious Incident of the Dog in the Night-Time** by Mark Haddon, which succeeded because it was unusual, accessible and page-turning. Anyone could read it and at the same time feel that they were reading something clever. It was easily marketable because it was unusual and high-concept; it sold well after that because people enjoyed it and talked about it. The Holy Grail.

Doesn't this contradict what I said about the importance of making sure your book fits a genre and labelling it accordingly? Yes, but there's a reason. Books that have such success are comparatively rare and because of this you should be cautious of calling your book "general fiction" in your approach to publishers. Only use it if it genuinely doesn't fit one of the other genres, but still ask yourself whether it is going to be easy for a publisher to sell. It must be piercingly and obviously original, perhaps high-concept. Classifying your book as general fiction without a very strong pitch or hook will do it no favours.

All books should aim to engage the reader but commercial fiction aims to engage more readers than literary fiction. Each genre has its loyal following and you want to tap into that. You want some of it. So, go get it. A literary novelist cares nothing for such go-gettingness but the genre writer must. You may not like the word "commercial", but if you write in a genre then you are writing commercial fiction, and that requires you to reach out to as many readers as possible, using all the knowledge you can find about how your own genre works.

SHORT STORY COLLECTIONS

It is notoriously difficult for a debut writer to sell a short story collection, because it is notoriously difficult for publishers to sell them in sufficient numbers. However, the writing of individual short stories is often how writers practise their craft and is a way to build up a useful portfolio of publishing credits[13]. It's beyond the scope of this book to talk about the rather particular techniques of this sort of writing, though there are some resources at the back. All I would say is three things.

The first is that your research into which might be the "right" publisher is more crucial than for any other genre: you must find publishers who have successfully published collections by writers who have not already made a name as novelists. The second is that some of what I will say about fiction in the following pages, on topics such as planning, plot and character development, applies to novel-writing more than short story-writing. If you know the short story craft, you will know that. As ever, adapt the advice to what you are doing. And the third thing is that if you publish individual short stories in magazines or online, you cannot necessarily use them in a collection, as a publisher would normally want the stories not to have been published elsewhere.

Even if publishing debut short story collections is so difficult, there are many other good reasons for writing individual

---

13   When you submit a book to an agent or publisher, such credits can be useful to show success – but only if the publications are genuinely selective and have decent reputations.

shorts: for practice, portfolio, self-esteem, experimentation or pleasure. And even for profit, though it's not at all easy to make a living in this way. Mind you, it's not easy to make a living as a writer anyway...

YOUNG PEOPLE'S FICTION

The most eye-bleeding mistakes are made by writers thinking they fancy writing for children. The thing is that too many people think it must be easy to write a children's book. After all, they're so short, aren't they? And we all read them when we were children, didn't we? Just how hard can it be to write a story about Pedro the Puny Pixie, tag a huge moral message onto it, slap in a few bits of heavy rhyme, and send it in an envelope shaped like a green felt hat? Possibly with some toffees inside because, of course, an agent of children's books must like sweeties. Oh, and pink confetti would be cute, too.

First, let me tell you that it's not easy. There are, if anything, more rules and more things to know about writing for children than there are in adult writing. And certainly more pitfalls. Under the canopy of children's and YA writing are many genres and sub-genres. And rules like tangled lianas, waiting to strangle the unwary.

COMMON REASONS FOR REJECTION OF A CHILDREN'S BOOK:

✳ Too wide a target age – although you hope that a wide variety of age-ranges will read it, you must target a range spanning no more than three years. For example, 8-10. If you say 8-12 in the query or covering letter, you mark yourself out as unknowledgeable. Yes, your book may be found in the 8-12 category in a shop and yes, it's a legitimate way to organise a shop and yes, there are books which appeal to a wider age range than 8-10, but the author, agent and publisher *need* more definition and precise pitching. Regardless of who *might* read your book, this is about who you *intend* to read it, and your average nine-year-old is a very different bag of bones from your average twelve-year-old. On the other hand, you may say your book is teenage or YA[14], without defining further.

✳ Inappropriate age of main character (MC) for readership. Your MC should normally be little older than your intended reader. So, for 8-10s you'd normally have an MC of around eleven. For younger teenagers, your MC would tend to be fourteen. Many ten-year-olds will enjoy reading about a fourteen-year-old, but a fourteen-year-old will tend not to enjoy reading about a ten-year-old. (Obviously, there are many exceptions, but I'm focusing on what the market and publishers require.)

✳ Inappropriate topic for MC or readership. Certain topics handled in certain ways are appropriate for certain age groups and the age of your MC will determine the topic.

---

14 YA stands for Young Adult. Teenage and YA are terms generally used interchangeably.

Your ten-year-old MC needs to do and think about the sort of things that real ten-year-olds do and think about. Sex, for example, would not be an example. Except in the jokey euuww way that ten-year-olds talk about sex, knowing nothing, usually, fortunately. So, the rule of thumb is: write about what your readership wants to hear about and leave out the rest, being guided by your appropriately aged MC. Since your MC and your reader may have rather different ages, it is not always straightforward to get the content right for both reader and MC and you have to be very in tune with what works.

* Wrong length for age-range – the higher up the age-range, the less strict the rules, but for young children the word count is tight. Do your homework: get some books for that age range and work out what is normal.

* Patronising tone or subject-matter – as soon as you start to sound like an adult telling a story to a child, you are being patronising. You are supposed to tell a story *for* a child, not to a child.

* Blatant moral message to teenagers or anyone older than about eight – when it comes to detecting moral messages, teenagers have the detectors of a shark sensing blood. Show someone getting knocked down crossing the road and you'll be told you were preaching road safety. Show someone eating an apple and you'll be told you're preaching about eating fruit. (On the other hand, you have to be careful about immoral messages, too… It's a tricky line to tread.)

* Wrong voice – "voice", as I'll explain properly later,

is "how the story sounds". Different voices work for different ages but must always be precisely right. If your narrator is ten, the voice of the story must be appropriate for a ten-year-old. However, it's not that you must sound like a ten-year-old, but that you must *not sound like a not-ten-year-old.* The voice must also be contemporary-ish but you should avoid using transient contemporary slang, as it will go out of fashion before you're published.

* Being old-fashioned – you may have fond memories of childhood classics but you can't try mimicking them. (Remember the Jane Austen delusion?) You have a choice: write an historical book or write a modern one. Being historically authentic is not the same as being old-fashioned. If you are writing a modern novel, your characters must be modern. This means that if they are of an age to have mobile phones, they either need a mobile phone or you'll need to show why not. This, frankly, can be an absolute pain in the neck and there's a limit to how often you can credibly have the characters being out of signal, credit or battery. Similarly, you have to consider that nowadays kids don't go into strangers' houses or cars, can't work in factories or play with matches; they wear helmets when cycling, elbow pads when skating, and can't climb trees without doing a risk assessment first. It was all right for Arthur Ransome and Enid Blyton but nowadays messing about on boats without adults just wouldn't be credible. And their damn parents are absolutely everywhere.

* Adults solving the problems. And other nuisances, like social services, who do a wonderful job in real life but are a menace for writers. Kids in real life have no freedom

nowadays, and this poses problems for authors. Hence the use of parents who are dead, feckless, drunk or scatty professor types; or fantasy and historical settings, where adults and social workers need not interfere and normal protective mechanisms can be ignored.

* A surprising number of mistakes are made by writers sending in picture books, a genre which is not nearly as simple as it looks. Classic errors include sending in a picture book text of the wrong number of pages or spreads, or with your friend's pretty illustrations; having too many pages or too many words on each page. Do your research: study the picture books being published now, analysing them in technical detail right down to word count. You will find they have set numbers of pages and far fewer words on each page than you probably imagine. There is a real art to thinking of an idea for a picture book and encapsulating the idea in lyrical, rhythmic[15], simple but beautiful prose that is wonderful for a young child to listen to and for an adult to read aloud.

So, do yourself a favour and do not think that children's writing is an easy place to start. The children's slush-pile[16] is awash with direness and I have seen examples which would, I hope, appall you. I know that you wouldn't write something so bad, but I caution you to treat children's writing with great respect and learn the craft like any other.

---

15   But, preferably, not rhyming. Picture books need to sell in foreign languages and translating rhyme is very difficult. Go for assonance and rhythm, rather than strict rhyme.

16   The mountain of unsolicited manuscripts waiting to be read by agents and publishers.

NON-FICTION

Non-fiction markets in children's and adult writing are wide-ranging and include best-selling books as well as more niche titles. You are fairly unlikely to make a great deal of money from one book but it's a very satisfying way of bringing your passion and expertise to the public. In the children's writing world, writers very often write both fiction and non-fiction, and it then becomes a way to financial survival, as well as something that many of us love doing.

Writing non-fiction is, as any writer should know, very different from writing fiction. The mental processes are different, the markets are different and the submission process is also somewhat different. The whole way of thinking is different. I wish I could think of a different word from different, but I can't.

GENERAL ADULT NON-FICTION

By "general", I mean not for the educational or academic markets. I mean books that you would expect to see in the non-fiction sections of ordinary bookshops. General non-fiction includes popular science or history books, biographies, how-to books, travelogues, cookery, and many more.

To have an adult non-fiction title accepted by a publisher, you need all these ingredients:

* Proven expertise in your field – supported by a CV showing the background to that expertise and a platform of some sort to show that people will listen to you. A

platform could either be an internet presence, including a wide network of contacts and potential readers, or a recent history of public-speaking on the topic. The fact that you've holidayed in Spain a few times and enjoyed a glass or two of Rioja does not equip you to write a book on Spanish wine.

* A "unique selling point" – a clear reason why this is different from other books on the topic. The point is that there are many wonderful and moving books on, for example, dealing with bereavement – so many that you must show why the world needs yours. So, it must be a) different and b) better or at least c) talk to a different and sufficiently large group of people.

* A proposal which identifies the market and the competition. I will come to this when I talk about the submission process.

* A readable voice – even if you're being authoritative, you can't afford to drone on like my old history teacher. You do not have the captive, terrified audience that we were. Also, although non-fiction has some different stylistic requirements from fiction, and often follows the rules of grammar and punctuation more formally, this does not mean that you should write like some rigid-spined Victorian essayist, carefully and pompously constructing a perfectly-formed though exhaustingly long series of connecting clauses so that your poor modern reader's brain is overwhelmed and your use of gerunds, subjunctives and absolutes and your refusal to end a sentence with a preposition leave him utterly unable to work out that

about which you were talking. In other words: write to communicate and engage, not to pat yourself on the back.

Quirky topics can do very well as popular non-fiction, tapping into the "what can I buy for my brother-in-law's birthday?" market, and, even better, the Christmas promotion market. An example of a recent well-reviewed, popular and expert book is Edward Hollis's **The Secret Lives of Buildings**. It's quirky-sounding but engagingly written, appealing far beyond the group of people who might have thought they were interested in buildings. It's a perfect example of idea, voice, and author platform, wrapped in one sellable package.

GENERAL NON-FICTION FOR YOUNG READERS

(By this I do not mean the specific educational market, which I tackle separately.)

Generally, children's publishers know what non-fiction they are looking for. Even if they are not educational publishers, they will look at the curriculum and identify any holes they'd like to fill; or they will want to update their list, as non-fiction often becomes outdated quickly; or they might have an idea for a new list or series. They then tend to ask their existing fiction authors, or send briefs to agents they respect. In other words, it is difficult for the unpublished writer to break into this field, because the chances of publisher A looking for precisely the book you happen to be writing are small. Since the publisher already has trusted writers, it makes sense for him to turn to them first.

However, children's publishers also want a pool of expertise in different fields and it is worth pitching ideas and offering expertise. If you write well and approach them professionally, there is a decent chance that they will take notice, even if they don't have anything for you at that moment.

A children's non-fiction writer does not necessarily need proven expertise in the subject. Of course, for some books it helps, and it is certainly important in some areas of educational writing, such as textbooks at higher levels. But for general children's non-fiction, the ability to research meticulously and write clearly and beautifully will outweigh academic status.

Children's publishers often produce non-fiction series. So, look at what's out there and see if you can come up with some ideas that would fit. If, for example, you find a series on common childhood experiences, and you notice that the publisher has a title on going to hospital but none on going to the dentist, offer that idea. But be careful to make it fit the existing format, including length and vocabulary. For example, look at the **Read and Wonder** series by Walker Books UK. It has a huge range of topics, in different styles, but the same number of pages and roughly similar word count. Notice also the extraordinary skill of the writers in that series. Children deserve nothing less.

Once you have your foot in the door, writing non-fiction for children can bring many commissions and be a decent source of income. Many of these will be based on a flat fee, rather than royalties, especially if they are within a series, but writing for a fee is not something to ignore. It is good for cash-flow, as you will be paid more quickly, and the income is guaranteed instead of being dependent on sales.

MEMOIR

What about the one subject on which you really are an expert: yourself? What if you have had a fascinating life and you believe the world would like to read about it? (Or, as is often the case, you have an older relative whose story you think is interesting.) Thing is, many people have had interesting lives. Interesting lives are an occupational hazard of being alive. And they are usually much more interesting to the people close to them than to the wider world. The crucial questions are:

* How interesting? Interesting enough that enough readers will choose to spend money and time on this book when they have a million other things to do?

* Interesting in a different way from all the other interesting books? How will this book stand out from others? The frightening truth is that the vast majority of books don't appear in most bookshops. So, how will this book reach its market?

* Can you write? Not just string some correctish sentences together but actually, genuinely engage your reader through the written word? Do you have style, a voice, and an ear for story-telling?

* Can you help sell it? Do you have a platform? Are you able to stand on a stage and talk about your book? I'll rephrase that: are you able to find an audience and then stand on a stage and talk interestingly about your book in a way that will persuade them to buy it?

It is very, very difficult to get a memoir published unless you are already a "name". I don't mean necessarily a celebrity, but someone with a proven record of interestingness. Or unless what you've done is exceptionally unusual and you can show that you can write and sell books.

A publishable memoir usually does more than simply record the story of the person's life. Think of Francis Spufford's **The Child That Books Built**, which is not only his memoir but an insightful exploration of what books do to us at different stages of our lives; or Joanne Limburg's **The Woman Who Thought Too Much**, which looks at living with Obsessive Compulsive Disorder. Living with an illness or disability is not enough unless it is unusual enough in some way, and also very well-written. Limburg's book ticks both those boxes: OCD is a condition which has recently become better known to the public, but there are not too many other books about the condition; and, as a poet already, she knew how words work. If, on the other hand, your story is one of depression, or surviving cancer – conditions which are the subject of many books – you would need a very compelling angle, and still need excellent writing skills. And beware: it's terribly common for people to think that their story or angle is special when it isn't. That's a very harsh message to deliver, but I am often presented with ideas or manuscripts by writers who have a story they are desperate to tell but which is just not sufficiently compelling to sell.

If you are not able to fulfil these criteria, self-publishing could be a good option. You will still need to answer "yes" to all the same questions if you are to have any chance of selling to more readers than your family, and you will have to work very hard, but writing a memoir is often more about creating a record of your interesting life than it is about becoming a writer, and self-publishing will certainly achieve that. Writing your memoir is often better treated as a worthwhile hobby, not part of a professional career.

EDUCATIONAL WRITING

By this I mean books which do not usually appear on the general non-fiction shelves, but which are sold directly to schools and colleges or to the specialist sections of larger bookshops, as well as to libraries. Educational writing begins with the very youngest readers – including those too young to read for themselves – and ends with anyone studying on any sort of course. It includes writing text books for specific syllabuses, as well as more general books that support curricular areas.

The educational market has been damaged in recent years by government policies of book selection, the slashing of school budgets and the rise of free online materials. However, publishers and writers who have managed to position themselves cleverly can still carve out a market. It can provide a reasonable income for children's writers. But, as with general children's non-fiction and for the same reasons, it's not easy to get into through the normal route of writing a book and sending it out. Educational publishers know exactly what they are looking for and when. They know what the syllabuses require, where the gaps are and what they plan for the next year. Therefore, if you've just written a fascinating guide to quantum mechanics, the chances of you sending it to publisher A at exactly the time when publisher A was about to commission such a book are tiny. And they are unlikely suddenly to think, "Oh, yes, quantum mechanics. Well, we hadn't thought of doing that but yeah, give it a go."

A better way of getting your foot in the door will be to approach educational publishers with a strong CV, letter and a sample of writing. Treat it like applying for a job that hasn't been advertised: you are offering yourself and your skills.

If you hope to write for very young children, you may not require specific academic expertise in your subject. For example, writing reading materials for new readers requires you to have an imagination, superlative writing skills, professionalism and the ability to follow a tight brief. It does not require you to have a teaching degree. A good educational publisher will have access to freelance subject experts who can check the book for problems. Often, the best person to write a book for the very young is a brilliant writer who is *not* an expert on the subject.

With text books for middle or senior school pupils, more subject expertise is necessary. For example, I would find it impossible to write a chemistry book, and most people without a chemistry background of some sort would be similarly useless. Publishers, therefore, want experts who can prove expertise, because that gives the book authority. Secondary school subject teachers often write text books. The more advanced the knowledge of the intended reader, the more you need to know, so there comes a point where high-level expertise is necessary. Having said that, a clever, well-read person who is a great researcher and writer can also carve out a successful career in educational writing. But be aware that a publisher will turn you down without evidence of your ability.

Whatever your subject knowledge, great writing skills are essential. Many terrible teaching materials have been produced by experts who just can't write.

If you want to get into educational writing, you do not need to write a book and submit it in the normal way for other books. Instead, contact educational publishers, telling them your background. If you've already written something relevant, show them. Suggest that you would love to write materials for them and offer to follow a trial brief. (Please note: if they use something you've written, you should expect to be paid.)

* * *

So, we've looked at what publishers think about when they decide whether you have written the right book, but what about the other range of reasons why they might still say no? Now we come to the question of whether you have written your right book *in the right way*.

SECTION THREE: WRITTEN IN THE RIGHT WAY

Your book might sound wonderful when you describe it to an agent; it might sound as though it would sell. But there are many things that could be wrong with it and many of those things will be enough to cause rejection. Gone are the days when a publisher might take a book with potential but lots of problems. Nowadays, for your book to be accepted, it must be in a better state of readiness than was the case years ago. Yes, many changes can and will be made during editing, but, the more faults it has, the greater the risk the publisher takes in accepting you: after all, what if you're not up to making those changes? Or what if the changes will be expensive in editorial time?

So, I'm going to shine my torch into all the hidden bits of your book, and help you find possible flaws. Some aspects – such as plotting and character – have had whole books written about them and this book cannot attempt such detail. But I aim to show you the possibilities and let you pursue them more deeply, using the resources at the back of the book if you wish.

For each aspect, you will have to use common sense to decide what applies to you. Some things clearly apply to fiction more than non-fiction. It should be obvious in each case, but I have also included some separate points about non-fiction where it seemed necessary.

It is your book. You should care for it more than anyone, like a parent with a child. But parents often don't see their children's faults. You must try to see your book through the eyes of others, or at least of the people whose good opinion you need. Eventually, this will mean your potential readers; but before that you need to attract the people who will bring your book to as many of those readers as possible: publishers.

So, let's shine a spotlight on your manuscript and see if we can find any room for improvement, before someone rejects it. Or, if they already have, let's see if we can find out why.

PLANNING

No one cares how or when you plan, but your finished book must give every appearance of having had a plan. It doesn't have to be written down, or mind-mapped in coloured ink. You could be like me: haphazardly scribbling on pieces of paper which I then lose; starting Excel documents with good intentions but giving up after Chapter Four; and having long conversations with my dog about what should happen next.

Do what works for you but do it because it works, not because someone else does it that way. Some people are prone to saying that such and such is the correct method; I don't care about the method as long as the result is perfect.

Possible approaches to planning:

* Control freakery – awesome planning in advance, with every chapter and episode mapped out in detail, accompanied by anal analyses of each character, including each person's favourite colour and what he would have for tea on Tuesdays. I am in awe of writers who can plan so intricately: I must try it one day.

* Inspired dancing with eyes closed – risky, because you can stub your toe, but fun. Not recommended for beginners unless endowed with mysterious genius. On the other hand, an element of abandoned bacchanalian dancing can be quite conducive to creative flow. Just be careful that it flows in the direction of a coherent structure.

* Planning in stages as you go, with a destination and a few stopping-off points in mind – pretty much what I do. It involves having certain desired scenes and objectives, possibly some clues about the ending, definitely a strong sense of what I want to happen, and then working out each bit as I come to it, but being open to new ideas as they occur.

* Reverse planning – this is my other method for maintaining a semblance of control and avoiding plot-holes later. It involves every now and then stopping and

making a fairly detailed plan of the story so far, tracing sub-plots, themes and character developments and making sure that I've not moved too fast or too slowly. This ensures that I haven't literally lost the plot.

But, however you decide to do all this, there is no doubt that your story must look as though it was planned.

NARRATIVE THRUST

When I ask agents and publishers what is most often missing in a story which is otherwise well written, one common answer is "narrative thrust". This is the force which drives the story forward, dragging the reader with it. You might call it page-turnability: the way your story makes the reader not want to put it down. I say "story", but non-fiction often tells stories, too, and non-fiction writers should be equally aware of driving the book forward and taking readers with it.

Although it's important in all types of fiction and much non-fiction, some genres require stronger narrative thrust than others. Katie Fforde, best-selling novelist of light-hearted romantic fiction and editor of the collection **Loves Me, Loves Me Not**[17], told me that lack of narrative thrust is the second "big mistake" that writers make when starting out in romantic fiction. (The first is to think it's easy.) Crime fiction is another genre where momentum is paramount. Perhaps it's these genres where we are familiar with the setting and personalities, and therefore need less scene-building, in which

---

17   published by the Romantic Novelists' Association

the emphasis shifts to plot. In fantasy writing, by contrast, the reader expects to immerse himself in and become entangled by the fantasy world, wanting to know and understand it. This certainly does not mean that a fantasy or science-fiction writer can afford to ignore the need for narrative drive, but it means that momentum is not as far ahead in importance as it might be for romance, crime, or thrillers. The difference is small, but worth thinking about.

There's a feeling, which I share, that today's readers often (but not always) require more urgency and momentum to the story than readers twenty years ago. You may not like this, but you should consider it, especially if publishers believe it. There's some evidence, anecdotal if not scientific, that we want things to be snappier, brisker. I know there are also modern books that are lengthy and weighty, but I am not saying that all readers *only* want snappy and brisk. I was certainly horrified to go back recently to some of my teenage reading and to find it too dense and slow for my twenty-first century mind.

Anyway, whatever the reasons and whether or not something has changed in our reading styles, lack of narrative thrust will often make publishers say no, so we must take heed. You want your readers to stay with you rather than drift away to the television or computer, so you have to keep them using the momentum of your story. This, above all else, is why I was rejected so many times and for so long: I was thinking too much about my pretty prose and too little about plot.

So, how do you achieve narrative thrust? There are four main elements: structure and shape; conflict; suspense; and pace. Let's look at each in turn.

STRUCTURE AND SHAPE

Stories have structures and shapes; they are not simply episodes followed by episodes until The End. Whether we have one single climax, or several smaller ones leading up to the big one, will affect the feeling of shape; whether the story moves smoothly towards the denouement or has bursts of action; whether the story contains flashbacks, whether it begins in the middle of action or builds up to it – all these affect shape.

No one shape is better than another. I suggest some possibilities below, but there are many ways of adapting these. If you want to understand shapes better, try analysing some books and see how they are done.

SPIKY LINES

I visualise story shape as a linear series of spikes, moving from left to right. Some spikes are small, others large, depending on how much tension I'm aiming for with each event. Although the spikes move up and down, the overall movement is up, so the line of spikes ends higher than it started. But the last movement is somewhat downwards, after the climax, the outlet of breath. In fact, each spike is like a breath. (I'll talk about breathing when I talk about pace.)

You might also choose a formal pattern. Humans like patterns and readers tend to like such structures, but you cannot force it, otherwise it feels, er, forced. So, only use a formal pattern if it feels right.

Here are examples of formal structures:

* Going backwards and forwards in time – as used by Sebastian Faulks in **Birdsong**, with sections named by the years: 1910, 1916, 1978, 1917, 1978/9, 1918.

* Regular switch of point of view (POV[18]) from section to section or chapter to chapter – this creates its own structure, which you can play with in limitless ways. Michel Faber's **The Crimson Petal and the White** is an example.

* A combination of time-switching and POV-switching – as in **Blueyedboy** by Joanne Harris.

* Seemingly unconnected episodes which the reader assumes must be connected in some way, and indeed will be. Kate Atkinson is a mistress of this and uses the device notably in **Case Histories**.

* A formal structure in two or more parts, relating to different time-scales or stories – as Sarah Waters uses in **Fingersmith** and Ian McEwan in **Atonement**. Emily Bronte's **Wuthering Heights** is another example of two time-scales within one story, achieving a different effect. Divisions into five or three parts work well – think of five-act plays, or the movements of symphonies.

* Having a prologue and an epilogue can offer a rounded whole, and this can be a satisfying and simple way to create a structure. It makes the reader feel that all this was

---

18   This denotes the person from whose viewpoint the story, or that part of it, is told. I talk about it in detail under the heading Point of View.

beautifully planned and it can create a feeling of, "Ah, yes, I remember that prologue now. How satisfying." Prologues and epilogues abound but if you'd like an example of where the device works well but has a different name, there's the preface and afterword in **The Moth Diaries** by Rachel Klein, where she appears to take the narrator out of the story at beginning and end, in order to tell us why she's narrating it.

✱ The story within a story – where the character has written or is writing a novel, for example, such as Margaret Atwood's **The Blind Assassin**. Or the main part of the story can be a character telling a story to another character, as in James Robertson's **The Testament of Gideon Mack**.

Possibilities are endless. Just remember that the movement of the story needs to be upwards, taking the reader towards a climax.

AND ARCS

You may have heard of story arcs? An arc is the term used to describe the *overall* shape of the story, the umbrella that covers all the smaller spikes within it. Perhaps the best way to picture this is to think of a television series where each episode may be separate but the characters also have over-riding events in their lives which are moving towards an ending. One test of a good story arc is comparing the main characters at the start and the end of a story: some change, whether external or internal to them, should have taken place.

The reason writing tutors go on about arcs is to get you to think of your story as having a shape, and not a straight line, not being too flat. Also to remind you that you can't end at a peak; the reader needs to relax. A bit like a cool-down after exercise, not that I would know much about this. As with the spiky design, an arc shouldn't have its top bit in the middle of the story, but nearer the end. Spikes or arcs – it really doesn't matter how you think about it, as long as you are visualising a good shape for your story.

I should also point out that the needs of different genres vary. In literary fiction, there is more scope for a flatter structure. Perhaps the changes in the story which produce the spikes and arc can be more internal or subtle, rather than external or dramatic. In commercial fiction, where the reader demands action and excitement, you will need a more exciting shape – more and sharper spikes, perhaps.

Whatever the shape and whether the shape is formal or abstract, by the end the reader should feel that the story is a rounded whole, however many spikes there are. The whole thing has to feel finished and as though it finished *there* because that was the plan all along.

NON-FICTION PLANNING AND STRUCTURES

It is hard to imagine how you could write a non-fiction book without having the chapters and structure mapped out in advance. There are many ways to structure a non-fiction book and you need to decide what's best for yours. For example, it could be chronological, or alphabetical. It could be structured like a narrative. It could start with the simpler aspects of the subject and move on to more complex ideas. You might set personal and general points side by side or decide to split the book in two. Your chapters might each have a summary at the end, or a quiz or a quote from someone. Very often, there will be several possible ways of structuring your book and you will have to choose what seems best to you.

If you look at the contents pages of a non-fiction book, you can usually see the thinking behind the author's decision. Randomly, I picked Nick Davies' **Flat Earth News** off my shelves. It's a book which seeks to expose the reasons why we can't believe much of what we read in the news. He begins with a story – our absurd worries about the "millennium bug" as we approached December 31st 1999. The rest of the book is divided into three sections, and the logic of it is beautiful: first, how the news machine works; second, how the hidden spin-doctors manipulate it; and third, some big scandals to illustrate all this. He finishes with an epilogue about solutions. Very clear, very logical, and containing its own narrative drive.

Since a non-fiction book, unlike a novel, may be offered to a publisher before completion, the full structure and chapter outline must form part of the proposal. The publisher needs to see which aspects you plan to cover and in what order. (But he might ask you to alter it.) So, planning is very important, even if the plan ends up changing.

Structure for non-fiction is not simply about the topics of each chapter. It also covers whether each chapter will contain some bullet-points at the end; whether tables and charts are needed; whether there are appendices, an index, a bibliography; and how you will organise sub-headings and sub-sub-headings etc.

It also sounds as though deciding structure should be easier than for fiction, but it is often harder. There are always things that could go in various orders and finding a logical and clear structure and then sticking to it without having loads of bits left over at the end, can be mind-bogglingly hard. My mind certainly boggled frequently while writing and planning (and re-planning) this book. If you have difficulty with planning yours, I suggest two useful strategies: put it aside for a few days or weeks and come back to it; and get someone else to look at it, ideally someone who would be an intended reader. I used both these strategies. Often. Some may think I didn't get it right but if you look at the contents list I hope you will see some logic.

There is one other important aspect of planning and structure for non-fiction books: what to leave out. You are not writing an encyclopedia – unless you are – and if your book is to stay on topic you must leave out what is off topic. Perhaps what is off topic could be kept for your website, like the out-takes on a DVD.

GOOD BEGINNINGS

It's an obvious truth that your first chapter has to be wonderful. It becomes especially crucial for an unpublished author trying to attract the attention of publishers, because the first chapter may be all they read. So, it becomes one of the most common reasons for rejection. You might think they should give you a chance and read further, but why should they? They will believe that *you* believe your first chapter is wonderful, so if it isn't they won't expect the subsequent ones to be better.

Besides, a reader won't give you the benefit of the doubt, so why should a publisher?

So, let's look at what your first chapter needs to do.

* Give a strong flavour of what sort of book this is. Sinister? Poignant? A thriller? Shocking? Light? Easy? Chicklit? Erotic? Historical?

* Give a sense of the setting, period and context.

* Not tell too much too soon; but tell enough. The reader should be intrigued but not confused.

* Introduce an important character – usually the main one. Make us care.

* Give tantalising clues about future action, elements which make it impossible for the reader not to read on. This will often, but not always, involve introducing the main conflict or tension. For example, someone is being chased, or a body has been found; perhaps a character's anger or hatred is revealed.

* Not give too much history or back-story.

A common problem with first chapters is the desire of the author to explain too much rather than too little. The knack is to give just the right amount, and your ability to judge that will increase as soon as you start to think about it carefully. Many explanations and details can come later and readers will have to wait for them. For now, they just need enough to be intrigued and not to feel blind-folded, but they don't need to understand everything just yet. Often, I have written my first chapter(s) and then gone back later and removed three-quarters of the text, slipping the necessary explanations into later sections. Sometimes, I've found I haven't needed to put them in at all, as the reader gradually gets to understand this fictional world for himself.

Every story has its own best place to start, and you have to decide what will work best. For this, you should not be thinking about rules: you should be thinking about story-telling and engaging your reader. I can show you some possibilities, and I reckon I've used all of them myself.

Some ways to start a story:

* At the beginning – including the lead-up to what will become the main action. For example, take **The Graveyard Book** by Neil Gaiman, which is about a young boy who grows up in a graveyard, cared for by the ghosts who protect him from a man who wants to kill him. The book opens when he is a small baby and the man is going to his house to try to kill him. Intriguing, scene-setting, suspenseful.

* Straight into the action. An example is the start of Pauline Francis's **Raven Queen**. "I am not afraid to die." (New paragraph.) "I have walked the three miles from Leicester prison, tied to a horse carrying two men who will hang me."[19] We will learn the reasons for this later but for now we are given enough detail that we know what's going on and want to know more.

19   Reproduced from **Raven Queen,** by Pauline Francis, by permission of Usborne Publishing Ltd., 83-85 Saffron Hill, London EC1N 8RT, England. www.usborne.com Copyright © 2007 Usborne Publishing Ltd

* Before the action, with an event which will inform the main story and which you might call a prologue. An example is **When Will There be Good News?** by Kate Atkinson, which begins with an event that happened thirty years before the main story. Her chapter is entitled "In the Past".

* The prologue for **Coram Boy** by Jamila Gavin offers another possibility: in the form of a fable, it is entirely unconnected to the characters in the story, but suggests the theme of the book – abandoned babies in the eighteenth century. The effect of this is that when the story actually starts, the author needs to explain less because we already know something of the context. (Some people get quite angsty about the virtues or otherwise of prologues, by the way. Quit worrying: if it needs one, have one. It's really no big deal. Or call it Chapter One if you're worried.)

* At or near the end of the story. Ali Smith uses this device in **Hotel World**, with the first chapter titled "Past". She even tells us on the first page that the story begins at the end. Beginning at the end needs careful handling, because the danger is that, since the reader knows something about the end, some suspense might be lost. In the right circumstances, however, it can increase suspense. If you choose this option, don't pepper your story with phrases such as, "As she would discover," or, "As I would soon find out." That would be too much of a reminder that you know everything and are simply dragging the reader along helplessly behind. Take the reader with you, not behind you.

Be prepared to change your beginning substantially when you come to re-write. I've spent far more time re-writing beginnings than any other parts, not just because they're important but because I often tell too much at first. I suppose it's because I'm trying to get my fictional world clear in my own head at this point; later, I realise that I've created something that didn't need such clear telling so early on. It can unfold gradually.

You must decide whether you want to draw the reader in quickly and dramatically, or to build up tension slowly. Whatever you decide, remember that at this stage more than any your readers can choose not to read on. When you get to the revision stage, be ruthless and ask yourself: is this really the best way to draw the reader in and keep him with me?

TIGHT MIDDLES

Saggy middles are common in first drafts but there are all sorts of things you can do to tighten up the core muscles. A saggy middle is very often caused by the fact that a writer powers into a book full of enthusiasm, and has that desired ending as a glorious beacon in the distance but is so desperate to get there that he rushes through the middle. You may wonder why this makes it sag – you'd perhaps think it would do the opposite. But what tends to happen is that the writer, with his eye on the end, lurches from episode to episode mechanically, without due attention to shape, suspense and reader emotion. The effect is that the readers' emotions sag, as much as the book itself.

A saggy middle can also be a function of a book being too simple. Do you lack a sub-plot, for example? Most books benefit from having a secondary conflict or storyline, different threads to provide variety and tension. If you have enough threads – but not too many, please – when you detect the imminent sagging of your middle, you can pick up one of them and give it some oomph, perhaps even taking it off in an unexpected direction. This has the effect of heightening the tension surrounding the main thread, while preventing you from having to spin out your main one unnecessarily – because it's the spinning out of the main thread that most often leads to the sagging.

So, although we often spend much more time thinking about the beginning, we can't afford to pay less attention to any part of the story.

A PERFECT ENDING?

Endings are so important to the reader and you will never please everyone. If you ask them, as I often do, answers polarize: some readers want a clear ending, with all ends tied up; others hate having everything tied up. Readers do want the ending to feel "right", though. They have spent time with these characters and they care what happens to them, but in fiction as well as in life what happens to the characters may not be perfect. If you have done your job well, readers believe in your characters, believe on some level that they are real, but you may have to kill a character or do something unpleasant, not because you want to make your reader unhappy but because you, too, believe in your characters and you know you have to tell the truth about them, even though in theory you created them and can do what you like. The phrase "right for the story" is one that we all need to hold tight to our hearts.

Guidelines for "right" endings – guidelines only, not rules:

* If you have lots of threads to tie up, don't tie them all up in one go at the end. Tie a few up earlier, and consider leaving one or two for the reader's imagination.

* If you want a surprising ending, fine, but you must have trailed this possibility earlier – it can't come utterly out of the blue because that would be cheating. It's fine if the reader says, "Wow! I didn't see that coming!" but only if he then says, "But I should have done, because now I remember…" or "…because it fits."

* Work out which of these words you will be happy to hear a reviewer say about your ending: satisfying, unsatisfying, intriguing, bleak, unexpected, strange…

* You have every right to make your reader feel anything you want. But they will remember you for it.

* Realise that you won't satisfy everyone. It's a tough world.

* If your book will have a sequel, this obviously affects your ending substantially. You need to be careful about what you leave unresolved: it's not fair to leave your reader without any satisfaction. After all, it may be a year before the next book comes out. My advice is that if you propose a series or sequel, each one should still stand acceptably well on its own.

As writers, we agonise about our endings but I suggest you don't fret too much. I believe that the place to consider whether your ending is right is in your heart and not in your head. You're a reader, too: does this feel right to you?

NON-FICTION BEGINNINGS, MIDDLES AND ENDINGS

Beginnings in non-fiction are just as important. In some ways, they are more important and carry a greater responsibility. What do I mean by this? I mean that the reader of a novel is usually there for enjoyment and will make a personal judgment as to whether this book will be enjoyable, based on the beginning; but the reader of a non-fiction book has usually come to learn something – even if also for enjoyment. So, if the non-fiction reader finds that it is quite different from the appearance of the beginning, he will be more disappointed.

I suggest that there are two main aspects to consider about the beginning of a non-fiction book.

* The reader uses it to gauge the voice of the book and to judge from that whether this book is for him.

* It must also give a strong sense of the level of difficulty and depth of the book.

Similarly, non-fiction books must avoid saggy middles. This can be difficult, especially if you have information which needs to go in but which doesn't feel as compelling as the rest. I suggest you reduce this information to a minimum and intersperse it with your more meaty content.

As for endings in non-fiction, readers need to be satisfied and to have everything rounded off in most non-fiction books. A non-fiction ending should be more like the conclusion of an argument, a real rounding-off, giving a sense that this subject is now well and truly dealt with.

CONFLICT – WHY SHOULD WE CARE?

Without conflict, there's no story. That's not quite true. I'll rephrase: without conflict there's no story that anyone would actually bother to read. Therefore, lack of sufficient conflict is a very important and common reason why publishers reject books. Conflict is the thing we care about, that threatens the main character, that the character struggles with. The reader's need to see the conflict resolved helps keep him there while you drive the story forward. So, whether it's unrequited love, unrevenged hatred, unatoned remorse, or unattained zen, conflict is central to your book and is crucial when you pitch the book. Multiple conflicts (within reason) are also a good idea, because you can solve one fairly early on, giving the reader some pleasure, but keep the others till later, ratcheting up the tension.

Think of conflict as the obstacle(s) in the way of your hero. The more daunting the obstacle, the greater the struggle, and therefore the greater the excitement and pleasure when the conflict is overcome. But don't think about this only in connection with your characters. You can have bigger conflicts, for example between races and religions, good and evil, male and female, emotion and logic, luck and talent, superstition and science – anything that's right for your story.

The conflicts must progress in a controlled fashion. Not in a straight line and not always in the same direction: setbacks increase tension. But you must be in control of how quickly, slowly, smoothly or bumpily your conflict develops.

The conflict should worry the reader but also create ambivalence. For example, if the girl needs to break away from the control of her parents, don't make those parents too starkly awful: paint different shades so the reader can see both sides. Things and people are rarely all good or all bad; things wished for often don't bring unadulterated joy; events feared may not be as awful as expected; death is not always entirely sad or survival entirely marvellous. Be subtle in the strength of your conflict and in subtlety will be your strength.

But the most important thing about conflict is that the reader should *care*. Different readers will care about different things. An eight-year-old child might care whether she'll be able to save up for a new Barbie; a grown man won't. This sounds obvious, but often writers pitch novels where I question whether anyone would care enough or whether this conflict is anything other than run-of-the-mill. Yes, I care very much whether my family appreciate the casserole I am making this afternoon, and we could well have major conflict if they don't, but that doesn't make it sufficient conflict for a reader.

Take any novel from your shelves and identify where the tensions or conflicts are: you'll find a great variety. The first book I picked from my shelf when I did this just now was **Regeneration**, the first in Pat Barker's trilogy of that name. This has many conflicts: between the classes, between the genres, between conformity and rebellion, and between insanity and orthodoxy, as well as the explicit conflicts between doctor and patient. Next to it was **Mister Pip** by Lloyd Jones, in which the conflicts are between peace and horror, a utopian life and a war-torn one, and between open- and closed-mindedness. But the conflicts don't need to be abstract. In Michel Faber's surreal **Under the Skin**, the conflict is in the main character, Isserley, in what she is, what she does and what will happen to her, murderous and tragic heroine that she is. In **The Hunger Games** by Suzanne Collins, the main conflict is utterly direct: which of the central characters will die and who will kill whom? But even when the main conflict is so concrete, there are other, abstract tensions regarding civilisation, decency, humanity.

Now, look at your book. Is strong conflict central and have you made it central to your pitch?

SUSPENSE

Suspense and conflict are closely linked. Conflict is what must be resolved in some way by the end of the book; the suspense is how the reader feels about whether, when and how that conflict might be resolved. I'd say that suspense comes from how you manipulate the conflict and the reader's interest in it. High suspense makes the reader desperate for resolution. So, we need to tease the reader, making him unsure as to what will happen. Suspense can be about the expectation of fear

– caused by the sound of footsteps in the dark, for example – but it's often just the manipulation of any expectation of failure or success. This manipulation goes a long way towards creating our intention of narrative thrust. (As long as the conflict is one the reader cares about.)

You can create suspense in different ways, depending on the context. Here are some suggestions.

* Slow down the action and focus on tiny details, just before something is about to happen. For example, supposing your spy is entering a venue where danger lurks, if you describe tiny details such as where he parked his car, an empty can rolling along the street, the narrow eyes of the doorman, the character slowly peeling off his gloves, you create expectation that something is about to happen. (If you then have nothing happening at all, you've cheated, by the way, and you can't do that too often without really annoying your reader. Yes, you can have a narrow escape, but not a complete anti-climax, because next time the reader won't believe your hints.)

* Insert specific objects which suggest important action. For example, if you mention a telephone, readers expect it to ring. This follows the principle of "Chekhov's gun": the writing rule which suggests that if you mention a gun early on, you must use it at some point. Since readers intuitively know this, even if they've never heard of Chekhov's gun, they feel suspense. Other obvious things which might alert readers to possible drama are footsteps behind a lone walker, a car with blacked out windows moving slowly, a power cut, a cyclist passing by unrecognised because of a dark helmet. All such details make the reader think something is about to happen.

＊ For more long-term suspense, as opposed to momentary flashes, you can drop hints to later disasters. The character on his first drug experience, the man watching the girl's house, the niggling pain or other medical symptom of a main character, strange behaviour that the character can't explain or doesn't notice – all suggest future problems or conflicts and help build suspense.

＊ Look towards the future. For example, you might start a chapter with, "When Jake woke up that morning, he had no idea his life was about to change." But be cautious about using this device. If you do it cack-handedly, it looks like a low trick and intrusion by the author. Is the narrator really in a position to know that Jake's life was about to change? You should be particularly careful if using first person narrative. For example, "Later, I would come to regret this decision." Ask yourself whether the time-scale of this story allows for such foreknowledge. The narrator can only look forward in this way if you've already explained that the story consists of the narrator looking back, rather than the narrator telling the story as it happens. For example, if you've said that this is the story of what happened to Jake one terrible summer, yes, you can use the device. But if you're telling a straightforward narrative, you can't suddenly show knowledge of the future. It has to fit the story.

Of course, some genres need more obvious suspense than others: psychological thrillers, for example. But you should think of suspense as applying in some degree to all fiction and some non-fiction, too. You can build it slowly, drip-feeding clues, or hit the reader with reasons to be fearful from the start. But, whether quickly or slowly, you must build suspense, because without it your book will lack that important narrative thrust. And then you will have given the publisher one reason to say no.

PACE – ARE YOU IN CONTROL?

The word "pace" is fairly self-explanatory. Speed. How quickly – or slowly, because slowness is sometimes good – the plot develops. Not all types of book need to be fast and not all types of reader require it. In a review, "pacy" is less a value judgment, more a statement that the book moves quickly. Yes, most readers like a story to move sufficiently fast, but a good story also varies its pace. So, one of the reasons why your book might be rejected is that you have not created the right sense of pace at the right times.

The most important thing to say about pace is that you must control it. You decide where and why you want some parts to speed up and how to achieve it. So, you must:

* Know what you aim to achieve with the overall pace.

* Decide where you want to speed up and where you want to slow down.

* Know *how* to do that.

Regarding the first point, this will depend on the requirements of your readers, genre and book. Some types of book allow a slower build, and attract patient readers happy to delve into details; others need a car-chase or murder every five pages. The pace of a thriller will be faster than that of a literary novel. Younger readers also need greater speed, less hanging around watching the scenery. The only way to know this about your genre is to read recent books within it – and you're already doing that, because I have nagged you.

Let's look at where and then how to vary pace.

WHERE TO VARY PACE

You will probably find it easier if you build this into your plan, even if subconsciously. If you are a formal planner, you can make a note of the places where you want to create change of pace. Or, if you're not a formal plotter, you will have to learn to get a feel for these moments, which usually come either just before or just after moments of great tension or drama. Here are some options:

* You have been building up to something, dropping clues, winding up the tension; now you create a breathing space, offering a slightly slower scene, trusting that your readers will stay with you, tormenting them slightly. This must be carefully handled because if your readers aren't entirely with you, they may lose interest, particularly if this is nowhere near the end of the book. Again, you must judge your readers and decide how much to let them relax.

* You are building up to something and then you pile in a fast, dramatic scene which the reader thinks *is* the culmination but actually there's more to come. So, a sprint at the end of an already fast race.

✱ After that dramatic scene would be a good place to have a pause and slow the pace a little. Readers will thank you: they do need to put the book down and go to sleep at some point.

✱ Certainly, after several scenes of extreme drama, you probably should slow down with a more gentle scene, before moving forward again into the tension.

HOW TO VARY PACE

Chapter ends and cliff-hangers

For me, pace is all about breathing and this is where you, the author, god in your own world, get to control a reader's breathing.

Think of one chapter as one whole breath, including the in and the out. You could start with the in-breath or with the out-breath, couldn't you? If you breathe in first – try it – and end with the out-breath, it feels complete, doesn't it? Well, that's like a chapter that finishes at the end of the dramatic moment, with the tension released. It feels complete. You could stop reading now and pick it up again later.

Next try it the other way round, breathing out first, finishing with a big in-breath. Notice that it doesn't feel complete. That's like a chapter that finishes just before the crucial event, a cliff-hanger, the reader on tenterhooks. No way is the reader going to put the book down now, not at this moment of tension, because there's too much urgency to know what's going to happen next.

Controlling your chapter breaks in this way is your most

effective tool for controlling pace. This was a revelation to me when I discovered it. By varying the point in the action where you end your chapters, you control whether your reader will be likely to choose that moment to put the book down for a rest, or whether he will be compelled to read on. Of course, you are supposed to allow your reader to rest at some point, otherwise you risk exhausting him, but you want him to rest at the time of your choosing. It's also worth remembering that readers don't like to be manipulated too obviously and may become irritated if you do this too obviously or too often.

Chapter lengths

The lengths of your chapters (or sections within a chapter if you have chosen that device) also affect pace. Short chapters create greater speed, a kind of breathlessness. I frequently use short chapters in my teenage fiction, because teenagers are busy creatures with many other things they might be doing, and need extra effort to tie them to their seats. Another method would be to vary chapter length, using shorter ones for greatest impact and pace.

Sentence lengths

Again, short sentences create a faster pace and help build suspense, especially if your other sentences are much longer. Short sentences don't only convey speed, however. They can also be an aspect of the voice you have chosen. You can use them for dramatic effect, too, as in Charlotte Bronte's "Reader, I married him" in Jane Eyre. So, be aware of the possibilities offered by varying your sentence length, and not only for pace control.

Sentence style and formality

If you are using a formal, strictly grammatical style, accurately juggling your subordinate clauses and phrases, incorporating participles and absolutes like a descendant of Cicero, your pace will tend towards something slower and more considered than otherwise. This might well be entirely appropriate for what you want to achieve. However, long, complex sentences offer a sedate ride, not a pacy one. While you can't pepper a Ciceronian formality with the literary equivalent of a high five, you will need to find a way to vary your pace by simplifying your sentences at the right moments.

Taking a break

After fast-paced sections, and before or after climactic episodes, taking a break for a more gentle scene can improve your book in many ways. The reader can reflect and process what has happened or is about to happen. You can show your characters in a different, more enriching light. Contrast also heightens the drama and gives your book an extra dimension.

The first time I was aware of doing this was in **Fleshmarket**. One of the (many) negative comments my irritatingly perceptive editor made about the inadequate first draft was that it was relentlessly grim. Bearing in mind that this is a book about death, surgery without anaesthetic, blood poisoning, filth, poverty and dead bodies, I took this as a compliment, but I also had to deal with it. One of my solutions was to take my two down-trodden characters up Arthur's Seat one hot summer's evening, where they made a fire and cooked steaks, breathing the fresh air and looking down on the distant grimness of Edinburgh. This offered the reader a break from the awfulness of what happened and made the forthcoming horror even more horrible.

PACE IN NON-FICTION

Because you are by now an expert in your genre, you know what level of page-turnability your readers want. If this is for the "popular[20]" market in your field, you'll want to avoid getting bogged down in too much laborious detail. Is this a book which you want your reader to rip through eagerly or to use as a weighty reference book? Is this a book with a narrative, such as a biography?

You can control pace in non-fiction with some of the same techniques as in fiction. Consider the following methods:

* Varying sentence length and controlling paragraphs.

* If your book contains stories as part of it, use story-telling techniques of suspense, just as you would for fiction.

* Be economical with words – just because you've done the research, doesn't mean it all has to go in. Too often a non-fiction writer assumes that just because the reader is interested in the topic, she is happy to read a long paragraph where a shorter, tighter one would have said exactly the same.

* Consider the use of footnotes in order to avoid holding up the text with explanations. On the other hand, too

---

20   For example "popular science" aimed at the general market, as opposed to an academic book for the academic market.

many footnotes (or, even more so, end-notes) hold the reader up.

VOICE

If you asked an agent or publisher what was the most common reason for rejection, you would get lots of different reasons. If you asked for the main reason why a book leaps out at them as being wonderful, you would most likely get one answer: voice. I hadn't a clue about this when I wrote my first published novel. One of the early conversations with my agent, as she was agreeing to sign me, went like this:

Agent: Of course, we'll have to deal with those voice slippages.

Me: Yeah, right, of COURSE. *(Exit far left to access Google).*

You may be wondering why my agent took me on if my voice control was inadequate. I can only think that she could see that it would only take a little bit of work to put the "slippages" right and that everything else was good enough.

WHAT *IS* VOICE?

Voice is just that: voice. What we sound like. When you and I speak, our voices sound different and our friends recognise them. We use different words and phrases from some other people, and we sound like no one else except ourselves. My voice can be angry, tired, bored, doubtful or sympathetic;

but, whatever my mood, it's my voice and always sounds like me and not you.

In the context of writing, there are two main types of voice: that of the author and that of the book. An author may or may not develop a distinctive voice which permeates all or most of his writing. Please note that this is not essential: you could be an expert in many different voices and certainly different voices are apt for different books. Many writers do have something distinctive about their voices, though, something that shines through every book. But it is not a prerequisite of being published. (After all, unless you are writing a series, the agent or publisher has no idea whether your next books will be similar or not, mainly because you haven't written them.)

Before I talk about the all-important voice of the book, I will say a bit more about this less-important voice of the author, because I know that many aspiring writers believe that they must "find their voice". Although, as I say, it's not essential before becoming published, it may be important to your confidence, to your sense that you have found the sort of book you want to continue to write and to the ease with which the words flow. So, it may be more important to you than to a publisher. It is also important if you're planning a series, because each book will need to feel that it was written by the same author.

Kate Atkinson and Bernice Rubens are two authors whose own language styles seem to permeate their books. There's something about the way each plays with language, the balance between the laconic and the brutal, something about the mordant language and content. In the case of Rubens, there's the explicitly Jewish voice that shines through all her work. But from the point of view of being attractive to a publisher, you don't need one voice permeating your work.

The voice of the book, however, is crucial. Your book's voice is its defining feature. It is what it sounds like, what it feels like, how it hangs together in tone and style. It means that you could extract a paragraph from two different books, and then expect someone to say which book each came from. It must be controlled right from the start. When you get the voice right at the beginning, the reader feels confident in you and is quickly drawn in.

A reader, even a reader who knows nothing technical at all, will notice if you make a mistake with voice, even with one word or phrase. Imagine you're watching an actor on stage and he keeps slipping out of character – you'd be tense and you'd stop focusing on the story. You might start to rustle your sweet wrappers.

Let's look (or listen) in a bit more detail.

The narrator's voice

Every story has a narrator. Sometimes the narrator is one of the characters – as in a first person telling. Obviously, if your story is a first person narrative, the voice of that character must be the voice of the book. So, if your narrator is a forty-year-old man with psychopathic tendencies, that's exactly what he must sound like, always. Everything about his personality must be reflected in the way he tells the story. Everything he says must be as he would say it. Alternatively, the story could be third person narration but told through the eyes of one of the characters. Again, the voice must reflect the character's personality and viewpoint. (Point of view comes into this and I will talk about that immediately after voice.)

But even if the story is not told through the eyes and words of one of the characters, the narrator does exist and has a personality. The narrator's personality is the voice of the book. Imagine turning your novel into a play with a narrator: the narrator would say everything except the dialogue. The dialogue would be in the voices of the individual speaking characters but the narration would have its own voice. **Blueeyedboy** by Joanne Harris is a wonderful example of a book with a narrator of chilling personality and a voice that sucks you in right from the first line.

So, when you say "It was a dark and stormy night", (even though you don't, unless you're being ironic, because it's a cliché) we must be aware of who is telling us it's a dark and stormy night. If you were to do a study of the narrator (even when third person and invisible), what would the characteristics be? It might be: young, old, fresh, light, delicate, sardonic, angsty, angry, formal, informal, direct, period, modern, witty, hilarious, offbeat, whimsical, sinister, unusual, poetic, ornate. Some or all of these words can also describe the style, and style and voice are closely connected but they are not the same. It's like the difference between what the actor sounds like – voice – and what he looks like or how he moves – style.

UNUSUAL VOICES

Some books have very distinctive voices. Distinctive voices are the hardest to do – hard to keep consistent and hard not to annoy the reader. So, they are risky, but satisfying to get right. Readers will remember them and publishers notice them. Examples where unusually distinctive voices have been successful are **Incendiary** by Chris Cleave; **Holes** by Louis Sachar; **My Name is Mina** by David Almond; and Lemony Snicket's books.

Then, of course, there are the books which break all the rules of our language and create their own languages, producing the most unusual voices of all, such as **Riddley Walker** by Russell Hoban and **A Clockwork Orange** by Anthony Burgess; or ones which use dialect for the narrative as well as for the dialogue, such as James Kelman's **How Late it Was, How Late**.

Don't feel obliged to aim for a highly distinctive voice, however. No one will reject you simply because the voice is not especially unusual. There are other mistakes you can make, and I come to that now.

CONSISTENCY OF VOICE

You can have any voice you like, as long as it's consistent. Read it aloud and tune in to anything out of place. Here's a tip: if one sentence leaps out as exceptionally wonderful (to you), it's likely to be in the wrong voice. The same applies if one of the sentences doesn't quite sound right. That's what my agent meant by voice slippages, and that's what I had to put it right. It's not hard once you start listening to yourself properly.

I don't mean that you can't have more than one voice in your book. I mean that within its own space – whether chapter or section – the voice must be consistent. You can have separate sections in different voices, but the reader must not be confused. If you picture your novel cinematically, you might imagine a change in camera angle, making it obvious to the viewer that we're now looking from someone else's viewpoint.

I do think that whereas you can juggle several points of view (which I'll come to), it's much less advisable to have too many voices. Unless you're very confident, I'd recommend not more than two, though each can reappear many times. (Many novels just have one. Two is not better than one – it's just different.) Of course, if your novel is meant to be avant-garde, risk-taking, different, ignore that guidance. That's all it is: guidance.

How can you make change of voice legitimate and obvious? You have some options:

* Change the tense.

* And/or change the font. Small sections of internal monologue, for example, could be shown in italics, but don't do this too much as it can become irritating.

* And/or make it clear in some other way that you've changed voice – for example with the chapter heading, or by indicating in some obvious way who is now speaking. It's quite common to alternate chapters between two characters, giving each its own voice and point of view.

Changing voice and not letting your reader know would be like having a radio play where you had two characters whose voices were the same, so that the listeners didn't know which one they were listening to at any given time. It would confuse the meaning and plot. You would be sent to the naughty-author corner.

HOW TO CHOOSE A VOICE FOR YOUR BOOK

It's often a matter of starting and seeing what happens. You might plan certain aspects of it – such as the age of the narrator, and whether it's going to be warm or light or friendly or witty – but the finer details won't be apparent until you actually start. Sometimes, when you start, the voice doesn't come immediately. Sometimes it comes naturally, which is the best and luckiest way, as it will be easiest to maintain. Often, the voice that comes when you start your book is quite different from what you intended. In that case, you have to decide whether to go with it or change it and start again. Often when a new book feels as though it's faltering, it's because you haven't got the voice right.

When you read a published book, you won't be thinking of any of this technical stuff about voice, because you don't get voice slippages in properly-edited books. (Unfortunately, it's a common flaw in many self-published books because far too many self-published authors won't pay for proper editing, partly because they think they are too good for that, and partly because they don't know how not good enough they are.) The slush-pile is full of voice slippages; it is a veritable morass of voices oozing and sliding all over the place.

So, some exercises for you. You thought you just had to sit there and read? Nope: writing is *serious work*. If it's any consolation, I wish I'd known about this ten years ago when I was still trying to work out what was wrong with my writing.

✳ Take the book you are reading – fiction or non-fiction – and the book you are writing. Look at the first chapter of each and analyse the voice. Can you describe the narrator's character and age simply from the tone of the narration?

✳ Pick one of these characters: tired old lady, bereaved man, baby, toddler in buggy, grumpy man/woman, harassed teacher, school truant, homeless person, bench/seat, road-sweeper, pigeon, cat, mother with three children, lost child, fly. Then imagine you are that character; picture yourself in a crowded place and write a single paragraph in the voice of that character, without actually describing yourself or giving obvious clues as to who you are. Give your piece of writing to a friend and see if the friend can say who or what your character is.

MODERN OR OLD-FASHIONED VOICE?

All your readers, of whatever age and however well-versed in classical syntax, are modern readers, because they are alive. But having modern readers doesn't mean we all have to write as though we're auditioning for a teen TV series. The language must be fit for purpose.

Different types of book require different styles of language, and varying levels of modernity and grammatical correctness. People of all ages, educational experiences and preferences will define and tolerate different habits and we all have pet hates. The more pet hates you have, language-wise, the more you might be drawn to write at the ultra-correct and somewhat old-fashioned end of the spectrum. I have a lot of pet hates – a hangover from my highly classical education for which I am grateful – but I also love the greater richness and flexibility which I see in stretched modern language; so, in my own writing I choose to twist a number of structures in ways which would make my Latin teachers turn in their graves.

What you cannot do nowadays, if you want to be published, is to write in a way which most people don't like. And most people now will not enjoy reading turgid sentences of self-conscious correctness; sentences which put grammar and syntax above style; or sentences which they do not understand because the writer is using an archaic form of a word. Words should be perfectly meaningful and beautiful. After that, your levels of correctness should be determined by what your reader wants and what feels right to you. If you have good control over your language, this is easy. If you don't, you shouldn't be a writer.

NON-FICTION AND VOICE

Voice is just as important in non-fiction, and much of what I've said applies equally to non-fiction, but there is an important difference: in non-fiction, your own personal voice is allowed to come to the fore in a way that would feel wrong in a novel. In non-fiction, you are not pretending to speak through the voice of a fictional character. It's one of the things I love about non-fiction writing: it's me, talking. On the other hand, for non-fiction writing for young children, this is not always possible. After all, the way I talk probably won't appeal to children and my use of the words "crappy" or "eye-bleeding eel vomit" is likely to bring the child protection people running.

So, your voice can shine through in non-fiction writing, as long as it is appropriate to your subject and for the book you are trying to write. For example, in order to write this book, I have toned down and somewhat formalised the language of my blog (believe it or not). Just as I would wear different clothes when doing a school talk from those I'd wear when receiving my OBE, I write slightly differently depending on my audience. Same with speaking: you'd speak differently depending on whether you were telling your teenage daughter why she should tidy her room or addressing the United Nations about why they should fight climate change.

Just as you must keep fiction voices consistent, your non-fiction voice must be consistent within the book. This means, in essence, that since I have set up a voice that allows the use of the word crappy, and lots of sentences that begin with "and", and various examples of colloquialism, I have licence to continue like this. This does not mean that you can't vary the mood, reflecting a change in topic. You can have variety without inconsistency. So, you can be serious and amusing at different times, but still write in a consistent voice.

An average modern non-fiction voice is very different from an old-fashioned one. Of course, many writers and many books still adhere to an ultra-formal style and, for example, would sniff at my use of sentences beginning with "and". And their readers will no doubt appreciate this. But language changes, and even pedants do not generally speak like scholars of the eighteenth century, though they often react sniffily against anything vaguely modern or experimental.

This is all about knowing your readers and being tuned in to what they will accept. It's also about being confident in your voice and language, so that you can twist it to your own ends.

THE CHARACTERS' SEPARATE VOICES

Within your book with its consistent narrative voice, you have characters who will each speak with their own voices – in other words, dialogue. Subtly, you need to make each character's speech authentic; but this does not mean that you should make them obviously different from each other just for the sake of it. Yes, an adult will sound different from a child and sometimes a character will have a particular mannerism to distinguish him, but don't go round tagging each character with some odd expression simply to make him sound different.

The main things to consider are that no character should say something in a way that he would not reasonably say it; and that if you have a character with a very distinct way of speaking, it must not irritate the reader. A pirate calling everyone "Me 'earties", for example, would be infuriating. Be subtle – you've got a whole book ahead of you.

POINT OF VIEW (POV) – HAVE YOU GOT IT RIGHT?

The basic idea of POV may seem simple: *through whose mind is this story or part of the story being told?* But there are some complications, leading to beginner writers committing "POV slippage". POV is an anchoring mechanism for your reader's mind. You control your reader with it. Get it right and your reader relaxes into the story; mess it up and it's discombobulating.

It makes sense to think of POV alongside voice. It's not the same but there are overlaps. The voice will to some extent depend on whose POV we are seeing the story from, and when the view switches, the voice may switch, too. Some of the same rules for controlling those switches apply. POV is somewhat easier to control, though, as it's easier to see when it has slipped. It is more black and white, where voice can be more subjective.

To be acceptable, a switch of view must be clear, deliberate and part of the overall structure of your book. Here are the rules. (And remember: they can sometimes be broken but only for good reason and with skill.)

* To be on the safe side, keep the same POV for a whole chapter. Alternating chapters with different POVs is one way to do it. (You can switch within the chapter but note the next point.)

* Always make it clear when you have switched. You might do this by choosing a different font and indicating through

the chapter heading, but you should use another device as well. It could be obvious from the change in voice; or you could make sure you use the name or something else that would alert the reader to the change of POV. Don't play silly buggers with your reader; it's annoying to be pulled up short after a couple of confusing paragraphs and to realise that the writer is now coming from a different angle. See **Multi-POV** below.

* Switching viewpoint should never be random, never just because you fancied it. It should be built into the structure. For example, it would be weird to have 99% of the book in Susan's POV but then suddenly, just before the end, insert a chapter with Jack's. But you could thread Jack's viewpoint through the book on a number of occasions, preferably with some sense of symmetry. Then it's not random, but structural.

POV slippage is when you fail to notice that you've just said something that the character in question could not have known or thought. An example would be when you are telling your story through Jemima's eyes, and you suddenly say, "Mr Green stepped off the bus, wishing he'd remembered his umbrella." The problem is that Jemima would not know he was wishing that. So, you'd need to change it to something Jemima could have thought. For example, "Mr Green stepped off the bus and straight into the driving rain. No umbrella, Jemima noted. Silly man."

My method of deciding viewpoint and working out whether I've slipped is to ask myself, "Says who?" whenever I'm unsure. Let me show you:

"It was a dark and stormy night..."

Says who? Who is telling us that it was a dark and stormy night? At the moment, it could be anyone. Let's read on.

"It was a dark and stormy night when Carmelle Jones pulled up in front of the grim little cottage, flung open the car door and tottered across the cruel gravel as fast as her Jimmy Choos would allow. The wind grabbed at her hair and rain spattered the notebook that she clutched to her chest. Cursing the impulse which had inspired her to sign up to a writers' retreat at this time of year – in the *country*, of all places – Carmelle rang the doorbell, shivering, dripping, and wondering just how long it would be before someone would pour her a glass of Merlot."

So, this looks like a third person narrative from the viewpoint of Carmelle Jones. We know her thoughts, at the same time as being able to see her from the outside. The narrator is not Carmelle, but is narrating Carmelle's thoughts while also being able to make observations about her appearance.

But here's the second paragraph:

"Inside the cottage, the sound of the doorbell woke Rob Flanders from a particularly pleasant dream as he dozed by the fire. An ex-SAS soldier, Rob always woke instantly, his ever-hard muscles ready for any action required. One smooth movement, and he was on his feet. He knew it was Carmelle Jones, of course. All the other writers had arrived. Soft and lardy, as usual, with arses made for sitting on. Too much laughing and weak eyes. Why he'd got into this business, he sometimes wondered, but someone had said there was money to be made from writers: all that poetic inspiration and not much sense, dreams of eternal fame and personal fulfilment. And he fancied a bit of smooth himself. Not that he'd fancied what he'd seen so far."

So, a different viewpoint. We're seeing the thoughts of two characters. This means it's looking like an omniscient narrator. OK, but the author – me – has to continue this. What I can't then do is have 95% of it being Carmelle's POV and every now and then slip into Rob's. (Not that I would want to slip into Rob's anything, obviously, but you know what I mean.) So, I'm going to have to keep it as an omniscient narrator, or alter what I've done, or have a deliberately mixed POV, which requires some special rules.

SOME POV STRUCTURES

First person single POV

First person narrative works perfectly in some cases and is simple to control. There are some disadvantages, however. The inner thoughts of one person can sometimes become rather tedious and angst-ridden, so you need to guard against this. Also, it can be restricting in terms of observation and description, because you are able to observe only what that character would observe. If your character would not know or care about the names of flowers, for example, you must either ignore the names of the flowers or, if necessary, have someone else name them.

If we have a single viewpoint, there are still ways of showing someone else's emotions. Instead of saying, "Jo felt angry," if the POV is not Jo's, we can say, "I could see the fury in Jo's eyes" or "her jaw clenched in anger" or "every muscle in her body tightened as if in anger". We can usually tell if someone else is angry but we can't tell the detail of their emotion. For example, you could know that someone looked "pale with hunger", if you knew he'd been locked in a dungeon for a day, but you couldn't know he was dying for a pizza. (This point also applies if you are writing in third person with a single POV.)

Third person single POV

This is sometimes called limited third person POV and it is probably the most straightforward and natural method. You would usually use the main character's POV. It allows you to talk about as well as through your MC. Of course, it does mean that you can't say what's happening when she is not there, but this makes it a very direct and natural experience for the reader because, if you think about it, that's what real life is like: we don't know what's happening when we're not there. So, the reader lives the story through one character, but not as intensely and restrictively as if it were first person.

If using this structure for a children's book, be extra careful to keep your third person POV consistent with the age of the main character. This is one of the ways in which voice and POV are inextricably linked.

Deep POV

I hesitate to give this its own heading, because it's really just third person single POV with a different slant, but some people are somewhat fixated on its specialness. I can best illustrate deep POV with an example.

Here is "ordinary" third person single POV: "She ran through the woods, as the wind and rain lashed the trees around her. She was sure she could hear footsteps but it was only branches snapping in the storm. She knew it couldn't be far now and she tried desperately to believe that was the light from the city in the sky ahead."

And here is the same passage written in "deep" POV: "She ran through the woods, as the wind and rain lashed the trees around her. Was that footsteps? Or the storm snapping the branches? Surely she must be nearly there. That light in the sky – that could be the city."

It's the same POV, but the "deep" view takes us more dramatically into the character's mind. One reason I don't treat this separately is that it's perfectly acceptable to mix deep and ordinary third person POV, simply using the deep one for the more dramatic moments. If they were truly different viewpoints, you wouldn't be able to do that with impunity.

So, think of deep POV as taking you further into the thoughts of the character, so that the reader can feel even closer.

Omniscient narrator

This is another third person narration, but using everyone's viewpoint. It should feel natural for story-telling, because of course the author is omniscient. Thing is, it's not the author who's telling the story: it's the narrator. And the narrator is, in effect, a character, even if invisible. So, it's not easy to pull off. The main reason for the difficulty is that if you are an omniscient narrator, you know so much of what is in every character's mind that there could be no mystery left – unless you are not going to tell your reader half of it. That's obviously the trick.

Another difficulty with the omniscient narrator is that some readers don't like it. Because we live our lives seeing the world through one pair of eyes, it feels more natural to do so in a story, or at least to see it through one pair of eyes at a time. So, for these reasons, it's one to approach with caution and to use only if it really feels right for your story.

Multi-POV – but not omniscient

This is a halfway house between single and omniscient which allows you to benefit from the advantages of each while avoiding the disadvantages. You could take one viewpoint at a time and use alternating chapters for each. Or much of the story could be through one character's eyes, with the regular switch to one or more other characters' viewpoints. This is a very flexible way of tackling POV.

Look at Neil Gaiman's **The Graveyard Book** to see the possibilities. Gaiman allows us to see the viewpoint of any character in the scene, or whichever one he wishes us to see at this moment, almost as though he moves the spot-light constantly. He is able to do this because he knows what he's doing; because he does it fluidly and regularly, not irregularly; because there's an element of traditional story-telling, in which omniscient and multi-POV narrators are common; and because it happens to work. He doesn't disregard rules, but uses them.

In short, for any sentence where you are not sure if you've got the viewpoint consistent, ask yourself, "Says who?" And answer it very honestly. If you can answer, "Says my intended narrator," your POV hasn't slipped.

CHARACTERS – DO THEY BEHAVE?

A story may be "things happening" but it is things happening to people. (Or, if you must, animals.) So, story is action perpetrated on and by characters; without characters all you've got is a car chase with no driver and no one to run over or care about being run over. Inconsistent characters or characters the reader won't care about are major turn-offs for publishers because they are major turn-offs for readers. So, let's see what you can do to make your characters tick the right boxes, so that poor characterisation is not one of your fatal weaknesses.

KNOW YOUR CHARACTERS

Your characters need to grow strong in your head before you can transfer them properly to the page. How you do this will depend on how much of a planner you are. Some writers have to know everything about their characters before they start to write. I tend to find out more about mine as I go but I can't properly start to write until I know two things:

* What they look like – I must picture them physically before I feel I'm with them. Until I can feel their personal space, I can't share it with them or see the world through their eyes.

* The main driving aspects of their character – because that is always crucial to the story and how they will interact with what I'm going to throw at them.

An important stage in the process of growing a character is when I learn Crucial Thing Number Two about my main character. It was my perceptive editor who taught me this. I've already mentioned my crappy first draft of **Fleshmarket**. Well, when I sent it to her, not realising that it was crappy, she said I needed to think of Something Else Important about my MC, Robbie. Up to that point, the only thing I knew or cared about Robbie was his situation of hopeless grinding poverty and motherlessness, exacerbated by having heard his mother's screams during surgery without anaesthetic. "What else?" asked my editor. The answer, or Crucial Thing Number Two, came to me in the car while listening to a Paganini violin piece on the radio: that Robbie had had violin lessons before his mother died and was desperate to play the violin owned and played by his nemesis, the callous Dr Robert Knox. Suddenly, a new essential aspect of the character provided an extra drive to the storyline.

I believe that every important character in a book should have a Crucial Thing Number Two and possibly Three. But no more. They can have many Non-Crucial Things, but not too many crucial ones. The second and third things enrich the plot in interesting and sometimes unpredictable ways and can bring your character to life.

Some writers construct elaborate questionnaires for their characters. This is not a bad idea, though sometimes the questions are plain silly. It is entirely irrelevant what my character's favourite food is unless this is going to come into the story. However, for those of you who wish to interrogate your MC, here is a questionnaire which might help nail your characters. Because I like reasons for things, I have explained the purpose of each question.

1. What do you look like? (As above – I need this before I can imagine them at all.)
2. What are your worst fears? (Likely to be part of the conflict and tension.)
3. What would you most like people to know about you? (Make sure it's obvious, then.)
4. What would you most like people not to know about you? (Every hero has a flaw.)
5. What would you most like to change about your life? (Could be part of the conflict and motivation; could be sub-plot.)
6. Why should we care about you? (Because if we don't, we won't read on.)
7. What were you doing before this story started? (This informs your back-story.)
8. Do people understand you? If not, what do they get wrong? (Makes your character more real because it informs interaction with other characters.)
9. What sort of people like you? Adults? Children? Male? Female? Why? (Helps place your character within the real world instead of just on the page.)
10. Are you happy on your own? (As above.)
11. What are you trying to achieve in my story? (Crucial for plot, since character drives action.)

12. What trivial but annoying habit do you have? (Makes character more real. Character can show this habit when angry/sad/stressed – helps you show without telling too much.)

13. What five adjectives best sum you up? (Helps you remember traits to paint most strongly.)

CHARACTER-PAINTING

Avoid chunky paragraphs telling us what your character is like. Delicate brushstrokes are what we want as readers, details drip-fed when we need them and not when we want to get on with the story. We do not want to think, "Uh-oh, description alert: let's skip to the action." So, don't go from top to toe, or even forehead to chin, telling us that your character has straw-blonde hair framing a delicately-boned face, a straight nose between almond-shaped eyes, and huge eye-lashes gently resting on a downy cheek. A clever writer throws out one thing at a time, beginning with the most distinctive ones – usually hair-related.

Although in real life we are not supposed to judge people by their appearance, in fiction you are justified in using physical aspects to enrich the personality you want to convey. So, if someone is a forceful personality, making them large and imposing, or very tall, or even short but with steely eyes and a strong hair-style, will help you convey the picture. So, choose what's relevant and useful – useful to you in conveying your desired message and useful to the reader in being able to form a mental picture. Of course, sometimes contrast is useful, but only if the reader gets it. So, if your steely sadist is a meek and drippy-looking figure, fine: say so but make a point of this contrast.

Different writers have different ways of deciding what their characters should look like and how they should behave. Some do it purely from the imagination; others might start with some random adjectives or traits and pick a couple to start with. If you have trouble coming up with authentic but non-stereotypical characters, I have a suggestion: use your eyes. Let me give you an example. I have, on occasion, succumbed to gym membership. (No, it doesn't last long for me, either.) Belonging to a gym is very useful for a writer, and probably for visual artists, too. Thing is, while you're tormenting yourself on a treadmill or something even nastier, you can be people-watching. Of course, you can also do this in a shopping centre, which is more comfortable and has retail benefits, but in a shopping centre you won't find people half-naked. The thing about them being half-naked in a gym is that you can see body-shapes more easily. The large cast of one of my novels is entirely filled with people from a gym near me. And no, I'm neither saying which book nor which gym.

As readers, we don't need much to get a mental picture: we don't need to know everything in order to fill in something appropriate. We just need the right framework. Take time over this. You may find you put in too much (or too little) at first – not a problem: it's called redrafting, folks, and it never ends until the fat lady with the cherry-red cheeks, piercing blue eyes and glossy black hair sings.

CHARACTER DEVELOPMENT – UNLIKE LIFE

One of the irritating conventions of fiction is that your main characters should develop during the book. Not just in the sense that we learn more about them as we go along, but also in the sense that they must change, usually for the better if they are the goodies. So, whereas in real life people very often continue making the same mistakes, in novels they grow and improve. And *you* have to control their growth. So, decide how, why and when your main character(s) will develop. Make this development fit appropriately with your plot and pacing structure.

CARDBOARD VILLAINS AND SACCHARINE HEROES

Characters need several dimensions. Bad people (in books) are more interesting when they have something that softens them, perhaps something that makes the reader almost sympathise, or feel that the villain is not entirely irredeemable. A bad character sometimes benefits from some soft edges that test our judgment of them. Anyone can do baddies, but baddies that challenge our perceptions and judgments are surely a more interesting thing.

Similarly, avoid the too-good. People who are completely good do not work well as fictional characters, unless they are minor ones. We have to feel we can identify and, if we're honest, most of us can't identify with angels. Victims in novels need careful handling, too – give them some spine. We don't root for doormats.

So, give your angels a touch of hell's fire and your baddies a candy floss stick to hold. Give all your characters depth and roundedness. Your book will be richer and more human for it.

STAYING IN CHARACTER

In real life, people often act out of character. So, you might think it would be legitimate to portray this in your book. Possibly, but only within reason and in context, and with care. If you keep making your characters behave unexpectedly, several problems arise:

* The reader becomes confused – and, although surprising a reader is one of the authory dark arts, spinning him round with a blindfold and then leaving him to fall into a pit is how you will lose him.

* The reader stops believing in, identifying with and caring about the character.

* The reader suspects that you are making the character do certain things simply to move the story in a certain direction.

If your character is meant to be irrational and unpredictable, make sure you justify this, otherwise it will look as though you stuck your plot together with flour and water paste. There are two main ways to justify a character's acting out of character or being unpredictable:

* By having unpredictability as one of his traits – though, again, it mustn't be haphazard.

* By showing that there is a specific reason. For example,

a passive character who hits someone might have been exceptionally provoked; or had too many drinks; or thought she was being attacked; or something.

DO WE REALLY HAVE TO LIKE THE MAIN CHARACTER?

Moot point. Personally, I'm happy not to like the characters I read about. Bernice Rubens is one of my favourite authors, and her main characters are often unpleasant and not the sort of people you'd want to spend much time with in real life. The characters in Iain Banks's **Wasp Factory**, a book I loved, were not exactly ones I'd want to hug. The main character in Gillian Philip's **Firebrand**[21], is violent, furious, damaged, and yet I defy you not to want him to succeed and survive.

That's the point: whether we like them or not, we have to care what happens to main characters. So yours can have flaws, but those flaws should not stop us caring. Caring about the character usually happens when characterisation is properly rounded, so that we can truly imagine that person, and when the conflict is sufficiently strong that we can imagine what it would be like to be in that position.

What we can't have, and what will make a publisher likely to reject your book, is a character who is dull, thin (metaphorically), incomprehensible, unbelievable, or half-drawn. As readers, we don't have to fall in love with them – though it's wonderful when we do – but we must have a connection between their hearts and ours. When this happens, we can forgive the character's faults and will him

---

21   He may change in subsequent books but currently I only have Book One to go on...

to overcome his problems, even when they are of his own making, because in the character's imperfections we can see, crucially, ourselves. We probably don't fully like ourselves, not every bit of ourselves, even the confident ones amongst us; so, not to like every bit of a character is not a problem, as long as we care.

SUPPORTING CHARACTERS

There are two sorts of characters who support the main ones. (Note: you can have more than one main character; or one main one and a couple of other very important ones who have major parts and are too important to be defined as supporting.) The two sorts I'm talking about here are the ones who simply perform the role of crowd scenes in situations where there would naturally be a large number of people; and the ones who are intrinsic to the plot, even if for quite small reasons.

Crowd scenes are difficult in novels. For example, supposing your book is set in a school or anywhere where there would be lots of people. You need to give the impression of lots of people but it would be boring to mention more than a small number specifically. The trick is to show your main character interacting with a few of them, preferably the same few each time. In the real world, your character would interact with many more people than you can afford time for in your novel. Paint the extra characters in small brushstrokes, giving the effect of crowds but without boring the reader with many names.

For example:

"The usual crush of bodies pushed through the doors. Jed could see Max and Joe further along the corridor. He tried to call out to them but two much taller boys squeezed in front of him. The noise was colossal. Someone's elbow dug him in the ribs and a girl with spiky hair scowled at him."

In that story, we now expect that Max and Joe will become more important, not that they will disappear and rarely be mentioned again. So, mention names only when the character is going to appear again.

Max and Joe will become the second sort of supporting character: people who are important to the plot because their actions will determine and affect the MC's actions. They may appear very often or occasionally. What they must not become is mere plot devices or ciphers. If they appear, they must do so for a reason and the reason must be strong enough. And the more they appear, the more they must become rounded characters themselves.

If your MC is part of a small group, such as a family, the dynamics between these characters need to be carefully handled. You need to select ages, genders and personalities to suit what you want to do with your MC. You have a great deal of freedom here but the choices you make will hugely affect the story, so get your choices right at the start.

Make sure that all your characters, however major or minor, perform at least one of these functions, and ideally more than one:

* Driving the plot forward.

* Getting in the way of the MC's journey.

* Creating or increasing conflict.

* Creating contrast with another character.

* Providing humour – if humour is required.

* Introducing a sub-plot.

* Reflecting or enhancing the setting, themes or story.

* Creating realism – as in my school example, or in any group situation.

SETTING – WHERE, WHY AND HOW?

Setting is more important in some books than in others. The place and time in which a book is set can become almost a character in itself, if you choose to make it so. But you do not need to. Your book is unlikely to be rejected on the basis of setting, but there are some settings more likely to appeal than others. And there are certainly ways in which you can improve the impact of the setting.

REAL SETTINGS

Just because you love your home town of Leicester, does not mean that your readers will care so much. (Apologies to residents of Leicester, which I know is a perfectly nice place to live – I am making a wider point and I needed to pick a name.) If you are going to make the setting central and important, consider choosing a place which will appeal to enough people. You might also wish to consider international appeal, particularly whether US readers will like it, since they are a huge potential market. I am lucky enough to live in Edinburgh, which is a wonderful setting for both historical and contemporary novels, and is a good example of a setting with wide appeal.

On the other hand, the setting could be deliberately unappealing. Meg Rosoff's **Just In Case** is set largely in Luton, and Rosoff told me that she chose Luton specifically for its lack of beauty and because it's a place her characters would want to leave, "like a springboard." She continued, "The town feels a bit like a gutted fish – with a semi-abandoned high-street and a pretty park surrounded by nice Victorian houses... and a massive flyover right through the middle that rips the place apart." See? So, I advise you to think carefully about your setting, and make a deliberate choice. It does also depend on how important the setting is to this book.

You must consider both residents of that place and people who've never been there and never will and remember that the majority of readers probably fall into the latter category. So you should not treat this like a tourist guide. Describe only when it's right for the story. Setting should be for atmosphere and character, and to help the reader, not because you were a town-planner in a former life.

If you are going to use real places, you must also get them right, otherwise you'll have Mrs Bloggs complaining. On the other hand, you can use a real place but make up a new location within it. Alexander McCall Smith's **44 Scotland Street** books are set in Edinburgh, where there is a Scotland Street but no No 44.

INVENTED OR NON-SPECIFIC SETTINGS

Sometimes, it does not matter to your story where it is set. And sometimes you do not want to specify. Perhaps you have a town in mind, simply to visualise a place for yourself, but perhaps there are aspects about it that you need to alter – for example, you might need a forest or a river where there isn't one. This is fine. But at least a vague sense of setting is important for the reader, so you need to decide the important aspects of what this place feels like. Obvious aspects include whether it's in town or country, beautiful or not, comfortable or not, the period and what country we are in.

There are other things you may need to decide in advance, and it does help if you secretly know where your setting is, even if that place does not really exist.

* How near is it to the sea? Do you need the sounds of seagulls and smell of salt?

* Or mountains? Forests? A river? Are any of these things necessary in your book or might any of them help?

* How far are we from the nearest city? If your book is set in the UK, much will be different depending on whether your story is near or far from London, southern or northern-hearted.

* Again, even if you know it's set in Scotland, for example, many things will be different depending on which bit of Scotland: dialect, terrain, concerns and weather will all differ. These all contribute to setting.

It is my view that you need to know, even if you choose to tell the reader very little.

DIALOGUE – DOES IT SOUND RIGHT?

Good dialogue is difficult and some writers are much better at it than others, just as some actors are better than others at doing accents. Good dialogue is dialogue that a reader hardly notices as good or not. Bad dialogue sticks out painfully, dragging the whole book down. Poor dialogue is certainly one of the things that can contribute to rejection, though it's unlikely to do so on its own.

The first thing to know about writing dialogue is that you should not try to write exactly as people speak. If you did, you'd have lots of *ums*, vast tracts of nothingness and many non sequiturs. At the same time, you can't write dialogue that the characters would never actually deliver. So, you devise a kind of stylised representation of speech, something that feels very natural. In essence, good dialogue is not about writing as we speak; it's about *not* writing as we would *not* speak.

Dialogue is usually best broken into sections, separated by narrative. You are not writing a film script or a play – unless you are, in which case you are boiling a whole different kettle of fish.

Some big bad things to avoid:

* Too many yeses and noes. Better to replace some with nodding or shaking of heads – though that can quickly become repetitive – or with the rest of the context indicating positive or affirmative.

* The blatant provision of information for the reader, which actually the characters would already know and therefore not say. For example, "Gosh, Sally, I hardly recognised you. You used to have dark hair with a fringe and now it's a blonde bob. Did I tell you I recently saw Samantha, your younger daughter, the one who went round Australia? Lovely girl. She's married now, of course, and they have a baby on the way." This is the author cack-handedly conveying information and ruining the dialogue.

* Dialogue tags – see below.

* Anything which makes it hard for a reader to hear in his head. (This means that using dialect of any sort is tricky.) You have to be very confident in your reader and in your writing to get away with the heavy use of an accent which that reader doesn't speak. Trouble is, sometimes it would be absurd not to use dialect to some extent, if that's how the character would speak, but do try to keep it toned down. Think of your reader.

✳ CAPITALS TO INDICATE SHOUTING. Or teeny letters to indicate whispering. Unless you think your readers really need and want it.

The key to writing dialogue is to read it aloud, preferably imagining yourself actually acting it. If you're not an actor, as I'm not, this is hard but it's the very difficulty which will help you think more carefully. If there's a bit of dialogue that keeps jarring every time you read it and you can't find another way to express it, turn it into narrative. Better no dialogue than poor dialogue.

"DIALOGUE TAGS," SHE SNEERED…

Dialogue tags are all the *he queried/expostulated/opined* bits that come between the spoken sections. Once beloved of Enid Blyton and many others, their over-use is now regarded as poor style. Perhaps surprisingly, it's usually better to repeat *he said*, than to vary it with *questioned, opined or muttered*. The main reason is that it's too easy to be tempted to *tell* the reader how the speaker spoke, but harder for the writer and often more satisfying for the reader when the attitude is revealed in action. It's just a bit lazy and spoon-feeds the reader too much. Don't feel you should *never* use tags: just be very judicious and, if in doubt, leave it out.

Let me illustrate with an example of an over-use of dialogue tags:

> "Do you want to come in for coffee?" she suggested.
> "Is coffee all you mean?" he wondered.
> "What else would I mean?" she scoffed.

"Well, just that I thought you might have some biscuits as well," he responded.

"Aye, right!" she laughed.

Do we really need any of the words outside the speech marks? No: we can manage perfectly well with just the speech, if the dialogue is strong enough. And that's the key: dialogue must be strong. Then you will need very few dialogue tags, usually only to show who is speaking. (Young children need more dialogue tags, as it is harder for them to follow who is talking otherwise.) Dialogue tags should show who is speaking, not how he spoke, unless that feels absolutely necessary.

Often, you can make the dialogue speak for itself, without any dialogue tags. Take a look at the same conversation re-written:

Carmelle looked straight at him. "Coffee?"

"Just coffee?" He stared back, streetlight shadowing his jaw.

"As opposed to?"

"Well, biscuits. I was thinking you probably do a mean chocolate digestive."

"Aye, right!" How did he manage to make the word *digestive* sound so desirable? Carmelle felt herself begin to blush.

Finally, just in case you haven't quite got the point, here is an example of too many dialogue tags with the extra burden of unnecessary adverbs.

"Listen," she whispered conspiratorially.

"What?" he interrupted eagerly.

"Nothing," she replied, hesitantly, deciding that she was not going to tell him after all.

And here is how you could re-write that without dialogue tags or adverbs:

> She leant towards him, her hair brushing his cheek. "Listen. I ..."
>
> His pulse quickened. "What?"
>
> Carmelle took a breath. She paused. What if her informant was wrong? She shook her head, looked down at the stem of the glass pressed between her fingers. "Nothing."

Please tell me you think the second one is better. Yes, the second one uses more words, but it uses them more powerfully. It uses verbs and action, showing us how the characters behaved, allowing us to feel that we are there, to experience what they do. It draws the reader into the conversation, relegating the author to a very appropriate sideline. After all, when you go to a puppet show, do you want to see the puppeteer?

OTHER POT-HOLES

Since I'm a crabbit old bat, I will now enjoy focusing on the other mistakes you might be making, things that make agents and editors roll their eyes and then dump manuscripts in the wood-burning stove. So, if you've checked all the points regarding pace, character, structure and the rest, why might your book still drown in the slush-pile?

OVER-WRITING

Over-writing means being over-descriptive, self-conscious about your verbiage, using long words where shorter ones would be better and over-complex sentences when simpler would engage the reader more. Over-writing means thinking of yourself, The Artist, more than the reader. It's often the mark of a potentially very good writer who hasn't learnt what to leave out. It can also be the work of a mediocre writer aiming too high and missing the target horribly.

The thing about writers is we're passionate about words. The trouble with passion is that we sometimes don't rein it in. I admit I'm guilty of this quite often. There are people in my life who restrain me, and very grateful I am to them. They are, in no particular order:

* My husband: "Shut up: you're banging on."

* My editor: "OTT"/"suggest omit?"

* My internal editor: "Do you really need *both* those descriptions you're so proud of? Go on: kill one."

I blame it on primary school teachers. When kids start to write stories, they're told to use adjectives, and adverbs, and multifarious detail, and the five senses; then they get onto similes, metaphors and other devices. When children use these techniques, praise comes their way. So they use more. And more. Some children don't, and no one praises them, so they fade into the background and become children who don't consider themselves writers. Meanwhile Arabella and George's stories are read out in class to demonstrate their brilliance. And so Arabella and George gorge on more adjectives and clever-clever literary devices, becoming carried away into some kind of ecstasy as they sit in their teenage rooms and pour their hearts into their diaries by moonlight.

Other kids are doing what other kids do, but Arabella and George are floating on moonbeams and dreaming fantasy worlds and the parts of their brains that are good with words become passionate about them and, lo and behold, two hopeful writers emerge and wish to unleash their talent onto the paying, reading public.

Thing is, no one has told them to rein in this indulgence. No one has told them that just because an adjective is beautiful, five adjectives are not necessarily five times as beautiful. Or that strong verbs don't need adverbs to prop them up. Or that words are valuable, and need to be chosen perfectly, that effort goes into the positioning of each word, and, crucially, its removal if it is not the best one for the job. (Note to any young writers reading this before taking public exams: it's entirely possible that examiners give extra marks for adjectives and adverbs, so please do not use this book as a pass-your-exam guide.)

So, grown-up now, Arabella and George begin to write novels. They write for themselves, because they must be true to their souls. They put everything into their oeuvres, all the power of language that they can muster. They read their work aloud, over and over again. They make themselves cry and shiver with the piercing anguish of their prose.

One day, they are ready to send their oeuvres off to publishers.

They visit a blog called **Help! I Need a Publisher!** – though they really believe that they should be on a blog called **Help! I'm a Publisher and I Really Need You, Fabulous Writer!** And they follow all the stunning advice about covering letters and synopses and sample chapters and tailoring the submission to the publisher. They don't even include toffee, or glitter, or naked photos of themselves, though George is tempted because he has a kind of Byronic air of which he is more than faintly proud.

And they are rejected. Because their work is over-written. The thing is that A & G, talented though they may be, are totally up themselves with the beauty of their prose and have forgotten that this is not about them: it's about the story, book and reader. Yes, we must love and believe in what we do, passionately, but if we put our pleasure above the work itself and the pleasure the reader will take from it, we may as well talk under water. If I sound harsh, it's because I am here to help you write a book which publishers will not reject.

HOW DO YOU KNOW IF YOU'RE OVER-WRITING?

Over-writing is easier to spot in others' work, because it's very irritating. When we find over-writing in someone else's work, we mutter, "OK, you really fancy yourself, don't you?" and it gets in the way of the story that we were trying to read. That's the main point about over-writing: it gets in the way. It hides the beauty underneath, covering it with frilly bits.

So, ask these questions when checking your work for over-writing. Ask these things especially when it's a piece of description, high emotion, or when you are feeling particularly proud of yourself.

* Does this sentence say the same thing twice? Or if not exactly the same then is half the description more powerful than the other half?

* Have you used three adjectives where one (or a different phrase altogether) would have worked harder and maybe ended up being more meaningful?

* Is this a bit where the reader doesn't want to be held back by description? Will the reader be tempted to skip to the action?

* Is this actually beautiful or is it in fact absurdly flowery? Are you being like a child who thinks that My Little Bride Pony is genuinely tasteful?

* If it is genuinely beautiful, is it in keeping with the rest of the book? Are you "in voice"? Remember, if the character whose POV it is wouldn't think like this, you can't write like this.

* If you've used a metaphor or simile, is it in keeping with the setting and period?

* Have you overdone the adverbs? (**Lazy Adverbs** comes straight after this).

* If you cut this paragraph by 25% would it be even better? (Almost certainly.)

Of course, the definition of over-writing is relative. Beautiful prose to one reader is self-indulgence to another. You have to work out where you want to be on the spectrum. Michel Faber is my writing hero – his prose is gorgeous, his imagination extreme and his vocabulary and imagery rich and rolling, yet he thinks about every word (or he seems to) and every word works. But much simpler styles can be equally impressive and powerful. In your writing, just make sure you're clear about what you want and whether your readers want the same.

Some genres and contexts require and tolerate more poetic bits. Some books and voices differ similarly. If you've read lots of books in your genre, you can more easily judge what is right for your book. But, whatever your genre, you will almost certainly do yourself a favour by toning down at least some parts, and then your best bits will stand out even better. You can't see purple against a purple background.

Mark Twain's words, written in 1880[22], bear repeating: "When you catch an adjective, kill it. No, I don't mean utterly, but kill most of them – then the rest will be valuable. They weaken when they are close together. They give strength when they are wide apart. An adjective habit, or a wordy, diffuse, flowery habit, once fastened upon a person, is as hard to get rid of as any other vice."

He's wrong, actually: it's not hard at all. Be tough with yourself and your writing will benefit. If in doubt, cut it out. My preferred weapon is a machete. It's remarkably therapeutic.

---

22   Letter to D. W. Bowser, 20 March 1880.

LAZY ADVERBS

Adverbs[23], used lazily, are an immature writer's stock in trade. Yes, they roll off the tongue, but so does dribble. The point about adverbs is not that they are intrinsically bad but that they are often over-used because they are too easy to use. Over-use of anything is monotonous. The judicious choice of the verb, or the context, is usually a more satisfying way to show the reader what's happening.

Let's look at some lazy adverbs. (I've put the adverbs in italics):

> She walked *slowly* through the woods, stopping *occasionally* to pick a flower, *sadly* thinking back to the time she'd walked here with her young daughters. Their cheeks had glowed *rosily* after a late summer picnic, and she could picture the hair sticking *damply* to their foreheads. The air had been heavy with birdsong then, but now the silence fell *eerily* around her and *suddenly* she felt a chill slip down her back. All things pass, she told herself, *reassuringly*.

It's an uninspired piece of writing in many ways and some of those adverbs are mere tautology, but the main thing is that they are lazy, for differing reasons.

✳ *Slowly* wouldn't be necessary if more care had been taken to choose a better verb than *walked*. It's not a

---

23   Adverbs do not always end in –ly, by the way. Adverbs are words which qualify a verb or adjective. So, "she shouted **shrilly**" or "her voice was **very** shrill".

major criticism, but I'd prefer something a little more atmospheric.

* *Occasionally* is necessary to the meaning, though it would be better if we actually saw her do it once and the rest of the thoughts happened during this one moment of flower-picking. If you think about this sentence hard, you'll see that the meaning is somewhat flabby: when did she do her thinking? Each time she picked a flower, or all the time she was walking? It would be more vivid for her to stop once and have this thought, and then continue. *Occasionally* is a cop-out here.

* *Sadly* isn't necessary because the context of the paragraph is sufficient.

* *Rosily* is tautologous after *glowed,* and *damply* is pretty obvious or would be unnecessary if the foreheads were described as *sweaty* (or something).

* *Eerily* is not too bad but I'd rather be shown other aspects that made me know it was eerie, without being told it so obviously.

* *Suddenly* should only appear when there is no alternative – here, it could be omitted without loss of meaning. Therefore, it should be.

* *Reassuringly* is the worst use of an adverb in the whole paragraph. The words that she spoke and the fact that she spoke to herself make it obvious that she was reassuring herself. It adds nothing. It's a horrible example of telling when the showing has already been done.

IN DEFENCE OF THE ADVERB

Adverbs are not bad; using them lazily is. Did you spot the adverb in that sentence? Should I have expressed that better? Differently? Ooops – "better" and "differently" – there go two more. Let me show you why it is absurd to claim, as people do, that adverbs are bad.

Take a sentence that I used earlier: "Adverbs, used lazily, are an immature writer's stock in trade." The adverb is "lazily". (By the way, "of course" is an adverbial phrase, as you'll see if you replace it with a true adverb: "obviously". Are you going to tell me that using it was *bad*? It's not bad, because it says what I want to say.)

Anyway, back to lazily. "Adverbs, used lazily, are an immature writer's stock in trade." Should I have avoided this adverb, "lazily"? If I'd omitted it, we'd have had, "Adverbs, used, are an immature writer's stock in trade" or, "Adverbs are an immature writer's stock in trade." But they are not. So it would be wrong. What I am trying to say is very simple: *Adverbs, used lazily, are an immature writer's stock in trade.* OK? There is no better way to express that sentence.

I should point out that some genres allow more leniency. The lighter, or more commercial genres, within both adult and children's writing, will tolerate greater adverbial profligacy. It is largely to do with style, meaning and prose skill, and nothing to do with faulty grammar. It is also an example of "telling, not showing", which I am coming to next.

In short, the careless or lazy over-use of adverbs is certainly a sign of weak writing. Certainly, really, actually, truthfully, adamantly, obviously, very much is. OK?

TELLING WHEN YOU SHOULD BE SHOWING

This is a thorny one. "Show, don't tell," writers are often told. *Told*, you notice, not *shown*. Well, I will show you that as a rule it's rubbish, but as a guideline it has some point. Sometimes a writer should show and sometimes it is better to tell.

By the way, no publisher will reject you because you've done a bit too much telling instead of showing, but it's something to watch out for in case you're doing it too much, as it will drag down your writing.

In non-fiction writing, you usually would want to state something obviously and clearly, so telling is perfectly valid, as long as your authority is clear. But in fiction we must leave something for readers' imaginations, for their desire to feel that they are exploring, rather than being led by the hand of a kindly but boring aunt. Also, even in non-fiction, we should not patronise the reader by explaining too much. "Explaining too much" is perhaps a better phrase than "telling".

REASONS NOT TO TELL TOO MUCH:

* You risk patronising the reader. Showing a character doing something, instead of telling us an aspect of his personality, gives credit to the reader's imagination.

* Showing can be more powerful. For example, you might tell me that Fred is cruel; but if you show me Fred ripping the legs off spiders and making a collage with them for

his sister's birthday card, it's much stronger and I know exactly what you mean by cruel.

* Telling is usually easier and lazier for a writer than showing. I have no quarrel with easier if easier is better; but lazier? Oh, I have a big quarrel with lazier.

* What often happens – and this is where critics of telling are at their most correct – is that the weak writer tells *and* shows. For example, "Peter had a headache. He pressed his fingers to his temples, trying to ease the pain behind his forehead." A headache? You don't say? This writer has told us about the headache and then shown Peter twice displaying his headache pain. Just one of these three will be enough, and I prefer the middle bit.

The decision about showing or telling requires you to have a keen sense of what your readers need to know, and to trust them. It's about thinking about your words and their meaning.

BUT SOMETIMES, TELLING IS BETTER THAN SHOWING

If, having read this book, including the bits on lazy adverbs and dialogue tags, you are convinced that you need to *tell* your readers something, do. Apart from anything else, telling is usually quicker, and quicker is often better. It's only not better when it's not better.

Take this: "Mr Johnson was a generous man, who would do anything to help people, animals, and, more than anything, his prize-winning vegetables." This is a perfectly valid example of telling being better. It's snappier and more effective than showing us Mr Johnson's myriad acts of kindness.

In conclusion: avoid telling your readers something if it would be better to show them something. Do not over-explain. Let your readers' imagination do some work, because that way they will engage more fully and deeply. They need you to open the door to the world, not lead them through it like toddlers.

SAME OLD, SAME OLD, SAME OLD

This is one of my pet tests for uninspired writing. It's also something which can drag your writing down and yet is very easy to deal with once you know about it. I'm talking about when a writer has too little variation in sentence structure. This is not to say that every sentence must have a different structure from the one next to it, but that too much similarity creates monotony.

The most common example of this problem is where sentence after sentence begins with the subject followed immediately by the verb. It's very little better than the "And then this happened and then that happened and then he said that and then this happened" structure of an eight-year-old.

Don't get me wrong: most sentences naturally work this way. Subject+verb+rest of sentence is the normal pattern of the English sentence. But to give your writing variety, richness and interest, insert other structures every now and then, even if only once in a short paragraph and twice in a long one.

A word of caution: in your effort to avoid over-use of the subject+verb start, make sure you don't replace it with the repetition of another structure. Otherwise, you'll end up with something horrible like this: "Running along the canal path, he yelled for help. Hearing the shouts of the men, he ran even faster. Panting, he felt the sweat pouring down his face. Nearing the end of the path, he tripped on a stone and fell flat."

In fact, even two of those structures would be one too many in that paragraph. There are many ways to re-write the whole thing. Here's one: "He ran along the canal path, yelling for help. Behind him, the shouting sounded horribly close, and he forced his legs to move faster. His breath came in painful gasps and he could feel the sweat and heat on his face. Still he could hear the angry voices, imagine the men's ugly faces. With a final effort, almost screaming with fear and pain, he reached the end of the path. His foot caught on a stone, and his body flew forward, landing with a sickening crunch." OK, not brilliant, but not monotonous in structure.

In short, listen for repetitive structures, although sentences that start with subject+verb can appear together much more often than rarer constructions. There really is no substitute for listening to your own work, especially after leaving it for a while and coming at it once you've forgotten what you said.

SUSPENSION OF DISBELIEF

The weird thing about fiction is that the reader knows that you are making it up and yet demands to believe in the whole story. Novelists can have impossible things happen, which the reader knows are impossible, and yet simultaneously you must make him believe that they did happen. A novelist can make a reader believe a character can fly, read minds, turn spinach into brandy, or live forever; but get it wrong and even the most ordinary and highly possible act becomes unbelievable, and if your reader doesn't believe something, engagement with the story is broken, often irreparably. So, the mysterious skill of the fiction writer involves making the reader "suspend disbelief", in other words to stop disbelieving. There are certain tricks.

Keys to suspension of disbelief

* Consistency of character. Remember I said that your characters must behave consistently, even if inconsistency is common in real life. If your character does something that he or she would be unlikely to do, just for the sake of your plot, your readers will see through this and they won't like it. They will stop believing what happens next.

* Consistency of magic. If you have anything supernatural in your book, the magic must be consistent. You have to set the magic up and give it coherent rules. The more wacky the rules, the harder they will be to believe. For example, a magic power that only works on Tuesdays between lunch and tea, and not if it's rained more than

three times in the last nine and a half days, and only if the empowered person had half a boiled egg and mango chutney for breakfast and washed her face in the dew while wearing blue chiffon, this is hard to believe. The reader will think you're making it up. Which, of course, you are, but not in a good way.

* Consistency of plot. Does this incident fit the storyline or does it feel out of place? If you have created your world well, and then you insert something that jars, we may not believe it.

* Reason. If you make it clear why something happens, your readers are more likely to believe than if you simply say it is so. For example, Jeremy's special ability to see the future could be because he is descended from a long line of wizardy people going back to the year dot, or because a special amulet was left in his cradle as a baby, or because … well, you get my drift: humans need to make sense of things, and when something has an explanation, we tend to believe it.

* Your strong narrative voice. If you have drawn your readers in and lulled them into a true sense of security through the strength of your writing, they will believe more. If you are all over the place, revealing your weaknesses at every turn, they will roll their eyes and accuse you of talking rubbish.

Important point: just because it has happened in real life does not make it believable in a story. If a reader says she didn't believe such a thing would happen, it is no defence for you to say, "Oh, but that did happen! In 1982 I was walking along…" It pains me to say that I fell foul of this while writing **Wasted**. There's a scene where a pigeon comes smashing through a window. One reader said she hadn't believed that bit. It was no excuse that I could truthfully say that this has happened to me twice: the fact is that I'd failed to convince that reader that it would happen. Slapped wrist.

This brings me to the use of random or chance events as plot devices. Of course, life is full of such events, but if they seem too convenient for the plot, your reader will not be convinced, unless the whole point was randomness or chance. The thing is that it is not enough that a certain thing could happen: the reader must believe that it would and did *in this story*. There are many extraordinary things that happen in real life about which one says, "If you wrote that in a story, they'd never believe you." Yep, sadly, it's true.

This, to me, is the whole magic and beauty of telling stories: the mysterious thing that our brains do to fiction, where we will believe the impossible and yet disbelieve the perfectly ordinary. The skill is in getting that right.

A SURFEIT OF BACK-STORY

Even if a story starts at the beginning of a series of events, at some point you will have to fill in some details which explain those events. You may, for example, need to tell us something about Alex's background or relate something that happened a while back. A character trait may need a reference to a childhood event, for example. This is called back-story. A beginner often gives too much back story too soon, or in over-large chunks.

Back-story is essential, but so, in my life, is coffee. This does not mean I should drink my daily five cups all before 10am. No, I should spread them out. Interestingly – stay with me – I tend to have nearly all my coffee before 2pm and drink other beverages from then on. This is only interesting because it is handy for my analogy: yes, your back-story should be spread out but it is also likely to be needed during the first half of your book more than the second.

Perhaps the most common way to overdose on back-story, and therefore the one to beware of most, is this: Chapter One, full of excitement and the clever trailing of intriguing hooks, with the introduction of a character we really, really care about and are desperate to follow; Chapter Two, a history lesson in which our main character's life story is laid out in meticulous detail. Result: either the reader skips it, or she becomes so disengaged that she couldn't give a damn about Chapter Three.

I have noticed something in my own writing process, and other writers say they do this too. I tend to fill the first 5,000 words with lots of explanatory detail, because I am trying to get the situations and motivations clear in my own head. Then, on revising, I cut a *huge* amount of it out, because I realise that as long as it all hangs together and makes sense, the reader does not need nearly as much explanation as I'd thought. In effect, the explanation was for me, not the reader.

So, back-story needs to be drip-fed, gently, so that the reader never skips over it and hardly notices that it's happening. I have come to realise that we need far less back-story than we often think.

POOR PUNCTUATION

I hope you haven't come here for a lesson in punctuation rules? That would take too long and you'll find plenty of places which will give good rules in books or on the internet. Punctuation rules and style also differ depending on the type of book you're writing and which side of the Atlantic you're on, amongst other things.

What I will say is:

* Punctuation matters for one reason: it helps the reader. It makes the text smooth to process and pleasing on the eye, and it aids meaning.

* Your punctuation style should be consistent.

* The occasional mistake will not matter but an obvious inability to punctuate will. If you are not confident, this is the time to call in an editor or competent friend.

* Avoid the "comma splice" – this is where a comma is used instead of a full-stop.

* Avoid exclamation marks unless you're shouting, exclaiming or giving a command. Do not use them

simply to show excitement. You may, however, use them more in dialogue.

* Get your apostrophes perfect.

EDITING ESSENTIALS

HOW TO EDIT YOUR OWN WORK

There are different ways to edit, but they all have the same aim: to make your book the best it can be. Let me tell you my core method and then offer extra things to think about. You can adapt to your own preference.

I have three stages. Stage One happens during the writing: I'm one of those continual self-editors, so, by the time I get to the end, I have already cleared up quite a few problems. Importantly, I will also have started making a list of things to change or check when I get to the actual editing.

Stage Two begins with a read-through of the whole book, acting on my list from Stage One. I call this the Silent Pass. (Editors talk about a "pass" as a read-through.) Gradually, the points are ticked off my list, although this always causes more to be added as I notice other things. At this stage, I am looking for large faults such as: plot inconsistencies, character development not being smooth or effective, pace, voice slippages, inappropriate POV switches, boring bits, threads that I failed to pick up. And small things if I happen to notice them, such as typos. This stage can involve several passes, because changing something can lead to more things needing to be changed.

Stage Three is the Reading Aloud Pass – I read the whole book aloud, at least once. Here I am doing three specific things:

* I imagine that my audience consists of a group of potential readers who would far rather be doing something else. My job is to hold them there. So, I'm honing my prose to ensure that each sentence, phrase and word works hard. If it doesn't, it goes.

* I listen for anything that sounds wrong – it's amazing how often reading aloud alerts you to a repetition or an oddity that you don't notice with just your eyes. Voice slippages and word repetitions are easiest to detect when reading aloud.

* I look for small errors and typos. Reading aloud and slowly, as though for a performance, helps me spot things that my silent reading eyes would have missed.

Stage Three can also involve several passes.

Other things to consider while editing

* To maintain consistency of characters, keep notes of all descriptions of them. This could be in a notebook or on-screen document, such as a spreadsheet. While editing, check against this document. I include actual quotes of phrases I use, so that I also don't repeat myself. "Eyes the colour of cobalt" is not a phrase you'd want to use twice

in one book, any more than you'd want to say that the eyes were powder-blue in Chapter One and mysteriously pond-brown in Chapter Eighteen.

* Consider using text-to-voice software, so you can listen to your text being read while you edit. Because it won't be a voice that's easy on the ear, you'll be able to focus on errors instead of relaxing.

* Use comment boxes or highlighting tools to raise doubts or remind yourself to look at something.

* Particularly for non-fiction, formatting headings and sub-headings is important. A publisher may well change all your formatting, but it's good practice to make it consistent from the start. Even for fiction, try to be consistent with paragraphing and layout of chapter headings. This will be your publisher's responsibility but it helps you look professional if you set high standards yourself.

* Printing a version is a sure-fire way to spot more errors. It's astonishing how different text looks when printed. There's something so final about it and it's that air of finality that can make the writer wince.

* Always keep an unedited version as a separate document, in case for any reason you change your mind about something and want to retrieve the original.

* Do it in chunks and pace yourself: if you spend too long at one session, you'll start to become tired and miss things.

KILLING YOUR DARLINGS

"Killing darlings" refers to the fact that we often have to cut the bits we like best. Why should we? Well, actually, we shouldn't necessarily cut them. We might like them best because they are brilliant, in which case they are allowed to remain. But the problem is that often we cling to beautiful phrases just because they're beautiful phrases, and their beauty blinds us to the fact that they don't fit. And if they don't fit, or aren't necessary or are just beautiful instead of being right, they should be cut, mercilessly. Killing your darlings is only a dramatic way of saying, "Edit, edit, edit."

WHAT IF THE FIRST DRAFT IS TOO SHORT?

Indeed, editing is not only about cutting things out. What happens when, after cutting out redundant words, you are left with a book that's too short? Or what if it was too short even before you cut things out? One thing's for sure: you can't just bulk it up with more description or character analysis or whatever. I have two suggestions.

Bring in a new character

What if a new character forced his way in? Right at the start. What if someone was watching your first chapter and muscled in? It could cause serious mayhem, in a good way. It could disrupt your other characters. There they are, all complacent, when suddenly someone from Carrie's past or someone from the future, or just someone with a new agenda arrives. It could be someone Sarah would hate or Emma would fall in love with or who would cause extra conflicts or obstacles.

Suddenly, your too-short book has grown volume, volume that enriches it and makes the plot bigger and better.

A delaying spanner

Maybe you had been so focused on the imminent ending that you hurtled your characters too quickly towards it. So, how about if, instead of having two things that get in the way of your main character's aim, you have three? Or four? Just as the reader thought it was going *so* well, you introduce a huge new spanner, and it throws everything into disarray. It could take another 20,000 words to get out of that.

Of course, there'll be more editing to do after that because then you'll need to do the cutting and checking again and you'll find bits that need re-threading and tweaking. But it will be worth it because eventually you will have your beautiful final draft.

BUT DON'T EDITORS EDIT?

When you have a publisher, you will be assigned an editor to work with you on alterations and to champion your book through all its processes. After editing, it will go to a copy-editor and then a proof-reader, who will between them expertly pick up the pieces of your sloppiness. But these things will cost time and, therefore, money, both of which a publisher would rather not spend. So, nowadays, assume that your publisher will like you more, and therefore be more likely to take you on, if your book does not require too much editing.

The three reasons why you should edit your work to the best of your ability are:

* Large systemic problems – such as weak characters or poor structure – will be expensive during editing because they will take time.

* Too many small problems – typos, repetitions, punctuation errors – make you look sloppy and unskilled as a writer.

* The editor might not believe that you are up to making substantial improvements. After all, he assumes you've presented this manuscript as the best you can do, and if this is the best you can do...

Certainly, an editor will want you to make some changes, even if you've presented a wonderful manuscript. Of course, no great book is going to be rejected on the basis of a few missing capital letters or a few semi-colons in the wrong place; no one cares about the occasional typo; and no one cares whether you've used US spellings throughout instead of British. But your passionate determination to be published and your own pride in your work should make you want to try your utmost to get this book right.

WHAT ABOUT HIRING AN EDITOR?

It is a moot point as to whether this is a good idea. If you are self-publishing, you absolutely should pay a professional editor, and a copy-editor and proof-reader. But if you are thinking of getting a professional editor to perfect your work before submitting it, you are treading a tricky line. Why do I say this, if a well-edited book is more publishable than an unedited one? It depends on how much the editor has done. If too much, then your agent will get the shock of his life when you present him with your unedited follow-up book and he realises that your first one was hugely improved by someone else. If you say that your book has been "edited", he may wonder just how much help you had and how much help you'll need in future. Something that you thought was a professional act could sow doubt in the agent's mind. So, I caution you to think carefully about what you want a freelance editor to do, and why.

I recommend that if you pay for an editor before submitting your book it should be for either or both these reasons:

✶ As an educational process for you, to show you major aspects that you need to address. The help that an editor might give you on an early "practice" book could be an invaluable way to improve your writing for the next one.

✶ When you have "finished" your book, as an extra pair of eyes to pick up typos and glaring errors. But not if those eyes end up doing too much for you.

An editor is a good support, but should never be a crutch.

If you want help improving your work, a better option is to get professional feedback so that you can learn to perfect your own work. I now come to this.

FEEDBACK

So, you've done all you can to make your book the best it can be. By now, you have probably lost all sense of objectivity. Sometimes you wake up thinking it's bound to be snapped up in a frantic auction; sometimes you know it's tripe. You need feedback. Even if you are quietly confident, you still need a reliable opinion. "Feedback? Chance'd be a fine thing," I hear you say. Indeed, it is hard to find when you are unpublished, though bad feedback is all too common. But feedback is well worth looking for and looking for carefully, with eyes wide open.

BEWARE OF PRAISE

Praise, like chocolate, uplifts the mood. Like chocolate, too much praise is bad for you. Praise from people who don't know what they're talking about can hold back your progress horribly and certain people are particularly unreliable in this respect. Unreliable people include your parents, grandparents, children, members of your writing group (see **Critique Groups,** below), unpublished writers, anyone who doesn't have publishing credentials or some other Reason to Know, most friends, and school pupils (who are great readers, but very unreliable witnesses).

I'm not saying you should ignore all praise; I'm saying don't over-value it. When you receive praise, ask yourself whether this person genuinely knows what he is talking about. Would he feel able to be negative if he wanted to be? If you think the person wouldn't have given negative criticism, his praise can't be relied upon. I see too many writers clutching at empty praise and ignoring the much rarer constructive criticism which could actually improve their writing and pull them towards genuine success.

CRITIQUE GROUPS

Tricky things, these. They are certainly useful for mutual support and for learning how to cope with not being published. Much crying on shoulders and sniping about publishers and weeping into wine goes on, and this is often important to your morale. Critique groups can keep you going or steer you in a better direction. At their best, they can provide eye-opening feedback and stop you making big mistakes.

But. A group's usefulness when it comes to feedback is often limited. Two crucial factors determine value. First, who is in the group? Specifically: how much do they know? How in tune with the market and your genre are they? Secondly, how is critiquing moderated? Specifically: how is constructive honesty ensured? How do you manage negative feedback, both the giving and the receiving of it?

Remember that a critique group has emotional attachments and psychological pressures within it. Can you give genuinely honest and near-objective opinions to someone when a) you are drinking their wine and eating their Moroccan chicken and b) they will then give you feedback on your work? There is probably also a hierarchy of success, with writers who have been published or come near to it, or who have won competitions and feel better qualified to give feedback. Some writers will be much better than others; but others may have more commercial potential. There may be personality clashes, which would matter less in a social group than in one where so much is at stake: the affirmation or otherwise of one's talent.

A well-organised critique group has firm rules about how feedback is given and received; members must trust each other, be aware of each writer's different goals, stay quiet when it's something they don't know about, be sensitive when giving but not over-sensitive when receiving negative feedback. On the other hand, if you receive negative feedback which upsets you, you need to be able to say – you should not just have to accept everything. Be clear about what you can take and what you can't and be sensitive when someone else shows signs of having received too much negativity. Members must be aware when colleagues have emotional or other problems going on in their lives at this time as this will affect how feedback is both given and received. To receive a very negative critique in the midst of an emotional or personal crisis can shatter a writer's confidence, so group members should be careful to manage the criticism they give, to make sure the writer is ready for it and really wants it, and to make sure that the reaction is not out of proportion. A critique should always suggest ways forward, not only highlight weaknesses.

Although I cautioned you to beware of believing praise from certain quarters, it is very important in a critique group that praise should be generous when it is earned. The concept of "earned praise" is a strong one and a critique really should start by highlighting the good points about a piece of work.

It's worth saying that there are online critique groups as well as face-to-face ones, and these can remove some of the pain of eye contact with someone who is panning your work. It means you can have your reaction in private, process it and calm down before responding. On the other hand, body language can be helpful, too, and arguments online can be pretty painful things because there is a detachment from personal contact.

Essentially, whether online or not, everything must be organised so that feedback is equal, open, supported and sensitive. If you can be sure of sorting these aspects out, a critique group is a valuable thing. If not, avoid it. You might consider instead finding – or creating – a writers' group which doesn't give feedback, just support and friendship.

EXPERT FEEDBACK

When you ask for feedback, you should look not for praise, but judgment. If you don't already have an agent, there are three ways to obtain expert judgment, including, you should hope, negative criticism.

Ask for it

You may know someone you feel would give strong feedback, perhaps a published writer or someone who works in the right part of publishing. If so, tread cautiously. Most of us shake in our LK Bennett boots when unpublished writers ask us to read their work. This is not because we're ungenerous. There are good reasons why we may be reluctant. If you are our friend, this could be the end of a beautiful friendship. I know many writers who have suffered in this way after giving feedback to people who said they wanted an honest opinion. Thing is, you want to be told it's brilliant. When we don't say it's brilliant, you think we're jealous or ignorant and if we do say it's brilliant, you send it to a publisher, who rejects it and you tell us we're idiots. Be aware that reading a book properly takes a long time. Finding a way to comment constructively takes a very long time, and more so if that comment is to be somewhat negative. Moreover, sometimes you will subsequently accuse us of stealing your idea. Please don't. I'm not saying it doesn't happen but it's like asking your friend into your house and then accusing her of stealing your purse when you just dropped it behind the sofa.

However, if you know someone you think you could ask, consider it. But realise that this is a big ask. You owe us a large bottle of champagne if the feedback is positive and two if the feedback is negative because it's much harder to give.

Pay for it

The second option is to pay for it through a writing consultancy. A good consultancy gives you a professional, expert, market-aware report on your work, along with advice about next steps. Different consultancies offer different services and you must choose one you trust. You need high quality criticism and you will benefit more from a really ruthless unpicking of your work than from someone telling you how wonderful you are.

Many consultancies claim to have propelled writers to publication but you should check these claims to find out exactly what sort of "publication". If the "publisher" was actually a self-publishing company, then this is meaningless in terms of quality. (Which is not to say that all self-published books are bad, just that paid-for publication is no measure of anything.) Investigating on the internet usually reveals any warning signs fairly quickly.

Another important aspect of a good consultancy is the pedigree of the actual people who will do the work. Are they substantially published themselves? Or have they had significant experience working in publishing, on the editorial side? A good consultancy will make sure both you and they know exactly how they can – and can't – help you, rather than simply taking your money regardless of the likely benefits for you. Not everyone can be published and no consultancy should guarantee it or even make it sound likely.

Hope for it

If you are lucky, when a publisher rejects you there could be some feedback in the letter. This is somewhat rare, as you'll see when I talk about dealing with rejection. But any comments offered with a rejection are better than nothing.

RESPONDING TO EXPERT FEEDBACK

If you send your oeuvre to someone you trust, don't reject the feedback when you don't like it. I don't mean you should crumple into a heap and gibberingly make every change suggested if you don't fully agree, but I urge you to consider the opinion closely and accept that the giver knows what she's talking about. Otherwise, why did you approach her, you fool?

If you agree with the criticism and it confirms existing doubts or produces a light-bulb moment, follow it. This is one of the best parts of the writing process: when someone opens our eyes to a problem and we enthusiastically pursue the solution. This has the added benefit that next time you come to write something you can use your new knowledge.

If you don't agree with the suggestions, you can't just follow them blindly, because it simply won't work. If you mildly disagree or are not sure, you could try following the advice anyway and see if it does help, even if you didn't expect it to. If you strongly disagree, or if it doesn't work, I recommend that you stay true to what you believe, rather than make changes that you fundamentally disagree with. Keep reading, learning and growing – sometimes, revelation takes time. Very often, taking a break from this piece of work and spending some time on something else provides the clarity we need.

And sometimes that clarity may show us that the giver of the advice was right.

IT'S JUST AN OPINION, RIGHT?

That's the common response of writers receiving negative expert criticism, whether paid for feedback or a rejection from an agent or publisher. And, of course, it is just one opinion. But, if the person giving feedback is any good, this is not just any opinion: this is an expert opinion. It is an opinion based on an understanding of the market and experience of how a book works and what ingredients will propel it to its readership and critical acclaim. It's also an opinion based on what this agent or this publisher can do with this book. A book is not just a clever idea wrapped in passionate words and tied with a pretty bow. It has structure and rules – which may be broken when you know how and why – and a shape, with patterns which are far from random.

Think of the TV series, **Masterchef**. It's a competition for seriously good amateur cooks. The judging is done by two culinary experts. (Then they shout; I wish they wouldn't.) Now, with food, it is literally a matter of taste. But when they judge, they are able to transcend thoughts such as, "Yuck, spinach," or, "personally, I prefer my steak really well-done". They have an expert view of what "notes" should be in a dish; they can tell you that each flavour is perfect but that there are too many flavours; they can say that the lemon is over-powering the rose and that a tiny whiff more cinnamon would improve it. They will talk about the shape of the flavour, the balance, the mouth-feel, the warmth of the salt, what it's doing to each part of their tongues. Now, call it pretentious, but they know how to judge food without letting personal tastes get in the way. It is a genuinely expert opinion, as objective as possible.

With books, true objectivity may be impossible, but an expert comes closer to it than a non-expert. That's what an expert reader gives you when finding fault with your manuscript. Of course, even an expert has personal tastes but a good critic will be able either to set aside those preferences or, if she really doesn't like this sort of book and doesn't feel able to be reasonably objective, to say so, preferably before reading it. Any expert is better equipped to comment on some books than others. You should choose your reader with that in mind.

If you take the "what do they know?" attitude to negative expert feedback, you risk missing not just the diagnosis but the treatment of your book's problem. Yes, get a second opinion if you wish, but take all expert opinions seriously.

CHECKLIST OF WHAT PUBLISHERS WANT

Bearing in mind that I've said that publishers all want something different, here's a list of the things they definitely hope to find in the next book they pick off the pile:

* A great idea, a hook which can be powerfully pitched in one or two sentences.

* A voice which engages the reader, is consistent and either feels wonderfully fresh, or is perfect for its genre.

* A book they can't put down – "unputdownable" is a cliché but we all want it.

* Something which booksellers will find easy to sell, because of the clear hook or because it sits nicely in its pigeon-hole.

* A manuscript which displays great competence in all the elements that come under my **Written in the Right Way** section.

* A manuscript which is not too far from being ready for publication.

* A writer who seems professional, sane and clued-up.

* A fascinating personal story or platform is an advantage but will not over-ride the quality of the book. Unless you are a plastic celebrity, in which case all bets are off.

Tick those boxes and there are only two more things to do. The first is to submit it in the right way.

SECTION FOUR: SUBMITTING IN THE RIGHT WAY

I hope you have not come to this section before absorbing the previous ones. It cannot be said often enough: it's your book that counts, not whether you drew smiley faces on the envelope. You can obey every bit of this section with sycophantic fervour but if your book is not publishable, it won't be published by any quarter-decent publisher.

However, once you've written the right book in the right way, how you submit it is important for three main reasons.

* You are sending it to someone who a) has limited time, b) has existing clients and books demanding attention and c) expects the worst, because that's what he usually gets. The recipient has a scarily low tolerance for crappiness.

* It's a highly competitive business and your book deserves the best chance.

* Only if a book is glitteringly brilliant from start to finish can you afford mistakes at submission stage. (Unless you are a celebrity, in which case you can write a load of drivel and not only get away with it but be lauded for it and have the plastic bits of your body photographed in silly magazines.)

Yes, sometimes writers break the rules for submission and get away with it. Go back to **Are rules for fools?** if you need reminding why this is a dangerous and pointless thought.

There are myriad mistakes to be made at the submission stage, and I have made many of them in my time, specifically during the many years in which I was failing to be published. (There's a lesson there.) Some mistakes are more important than others. You should attempt to avoid all of them but if you discover too late that you've done something wrong, don't lose any sleep: agents and publishers are not vile creatures who are desperate for you to mess up. They actually do want your book to be wonderful and they will overlook minor transgressions if your book is good enough.

The first thing to remember is that the vast majority of submissions are appalling. Really. Agents show me stuff they've been sent. They laugh – whereas I, having an embarrassing past, merely wince. For a novice, some of the traps are easy to fall into, but also easy to avoid once you know about them.

GENERAL BASICS

AGENTS

Over the years of being published by different publishers in different genres, I have gleaned some knowledge about contracts and rights and how to fight for mine. Yet, if my agent decided to hang up her stilettos, I'd throw myself at the feet of another. Why? In short, because I want to write, not fight for my rights. And my agent, as all good agents will, does all the things listed below and does them so much better than I could. Since agents only earn a percentage of their clients' income, they have a vested interest in maximizing that income. That seems to me not a bad thing.

WHAT A GOOD AGENT DOES

* Gives honest, expert feedback on your work, and makes you improve it if necessary – lessening the chance of rejection and egg on your face.

* Knows where to send your work – including individual editors and their preferences – and sends it for you, so you never have to worry about a submission again; discusses you with publishers who trust her judgment.

* Negotiates the best deal, including every aspect of the contract, having a finger on the pulse of what other agents

are negotiating, especially in the changing arena of digital rights etc.

* Sells subsidiary rights – such as foreign, film and TV, and audio.

* Understands royalty statements and queries them if necessary – royalty statements are a minefield for writers. I tend to come over all faint when I see them.

* Has an eye for new opportunities – publishers, particularly in educational and children's markets, will tell agents what they are looking for and your agent can pass this information to you.

* Manages your long-term career, guiding you in sensible directions.

* Deals with problems, niggles and disasters. These things will happen.

* Plays bad cop with your publisher, so that you can play the part of lovely, calm, reasonable author.

* Increases your earnings – authors with agents earn more than those without.

* Allows you to write.

Some agents do the following as well, but most don't:

* Create publicity for you – other than the obvious plugging of your name where possible.

* Organise your event programme.

* Edit your work – all agents should suggest important alterations, but detailed editing is not their normal job, unless they actually say it is.

You will hear people say that agents are sharks and will drink your blood dry. As with all professions, the bad drag down the reputations of the good. Find yourself a good one – following the advice on the following pages – and you won't regret it.

YOU DO NOT ACTUALLY NEED AN AGENT

Despite what I have just said, many writers manage well without an agent. If you don't have an agent, either through choice or necessity, note the following:

* The Society of Authors provides very useful leaflets covering all aspects of contracts. **The Writer's Handbook** and the **Writers' and Artists' Yearbook** also contain invaluable advice.

* Once you are offered a publishing contract, join the Society of Authors because they provide a free contract vetting service.

* Consider joining other authors, through a writing group, to share knowledge and experiences. If you can't find a group, set one up.

* Get plugged in to such things as blogging and Twitter, because the more writers you know, the better armed you will be.

WHO CAN'T HAVE AN AGENT?

If your future earnings are likely to be very small and you are not focused on a long-term career, you will be unlikely to find an agent.

Reasons include:

* You are a poet. It is nigh-on impossible to earn a living as a poet, except through performance, in which the agent is unlikely to share.

* You have a one-off book and no intention of writing more in the same genre.

* You are a non-fiction writer. Many non-fiction writers do have agents but, again, you'd need to look as though this was going to be a career for you, with many ideas for future books.

* You are…brace yourself…too old. Yes, I am sorry about this, but it's the long-term career problem. However, there is no hard and fast rule about what is "too old" and it does, as ever, depend on the book. If your book is wonderful and looks as though it could sell in big numbers, you can still attract an agent. Also, the age at which it becomes harder to start a writing career is greater than for other careers. After all, if you are sixty and you're

good enough, you've still got enough years ahead of you to make a pretty good career.

RESEARCH BEFORE SUBMISSION

A great deal of time is wasted by writers sending stuff to the wrong people and there is much to be learnt from some simple research:

* What sort of books they represent or publish. No agent or publisher deals with every type of book and you're wasting your time if you send to the wrong ones.

* Individual submission guidelines.

* The quality and professionalism of the agent or publisher, which will make all the difference to your career. With the agent, find out what clients he has and how successful they are. If he's brand new, ask what experience of the publishing industry he has; if it's slim, do not touch with a barge-pole. (See **Beware crappy agents**.) With the publisher, make sure that the books look good, and sell reasonably widely. (See **And crappy publishers**.)

* Whether you are proposing a directly competing series. If you have a series about bad fairies, you don't want to send it to the publisher of an existing (and therefore rival) bad fairy series.

So, this is partly about making sure you end up with a good

publisher or agent and partly about not wasting your time by approaching those who don't handle your sort of book.

BEWARE CRAPPY AGENTS

I know that if Godzilla, egged on by a Dalek, lumbered into your garden and offered to be your agent, get you published and make you a millionaire, you'd agree. You'd even ignore the millionaire bit. You'd certainly ignore the mad look in his eyes and the fact that he's never sold a book in his life.

Thing is, anyone can be an agent. There's no exam. And I have heard terrible stories: Godzilla is cuddly by comparison. Since a great deal of awfulness could happen if you get this wrong, I need you to know how to choose a proper agent. A bad agent is much worse than no agent, destroying your career before it has started and leaving you more stressed than you can imagine an unpublished writer could be. As if being unpublished weren't stressful enough.

Once an agent has expressed a desire to represent you, before you get into bed with him – I am not being literal – you need to exercise due diligence. Here are some questions to separate the rancid cream from the yogurt; some you must ask directly, while others you may find out through asking around:

* What other authors does the agent represent? (Check that these authors are properly published and have some success.)

* What previous experience of publishing led to his

becoming an agent? (If there is no previous proper experience, run.)

* Is this the agent's only job? (If not, how serious is he and how much time and energy will the agent have for you?)

* How does the agent sell foreign rights? For example, he might use sub-agents or scouts, but there should be some clear answer to the question. (Similar question for TV/film rights, and merchandising rights if you write for young children. But avoid sounding as though you think your book merits TV/film/merchandising opportunities.)

* Is the agent a member of the Association of Authors' Agents[24]? (It's not essential to be a member, and smaller independent agents often aren't, but you should ask if the agent at least adheres to its code of practice, a code which you can read on the AAA website.) In Scotland there's also the Association of Scottish Literary Agents.

* Can you see the contract that you would sign? Get it checked by someone who understands: perhaps another agented author, or the Society of Authors if you are a member.

* Is the agent asking for money up front? If so, run a mile. An agent should not charge a reading fee, though they are quite entitled to charge for things like photo-copying. Such extras should be specified in the contract.

Being an agent is not a job for amateurs. Obviously, every

---

24   agentsassoc.co.uk

agent must start somewhere and acquire a first client – but this can only work if that agent already has substantial experience of dealing with publishing rights in another professional capacity. For example, many agents were publishers for years before they became agents and that is a good way into the business.

It's also important that you actually like the agent. A perfectly brilliant agent simply might not be right for you and it's important to allow instinct to come into play. So, meet your agent if possible. At the very least, have some phone conversations and remain sober during them.

In short, be astute and cautious. Think Godzilla.

AND CRAPPY PUBLISHERS

If you're struggling to be published, you perhaps don't care which publisher takes you on, as long as someone does. You *should* care and I urge you to investigate carefully. Luckily, thanks to the internet, it is simple to investigate the reputation of your proposed publisher. So, do a search. First, search the term "[insert name of publisher] + scam". Some companies call themselves publishers and will try to make you think they are using the traditional model of selective publishing with an editing process and that they will sell your book, whereas in fact they make their money from the author and will do nothing to make your book look good because they do not make their profit from selling it. (That's how you tell the difference: who pays and who is paid? If the author pays at any stage, it's paid-for publishing. According to Yog's

Law[25], money is supposed to flow to the author, not from the author.) There are horrible scams out there and I know many sad stories of fooled writers who think they are published when they are merely printed, at their own cost.

Once you're reassured that there are no scam-related reasons to avoid this company, find some of their books and see what you think of them. Production quality is important: readers generally like books to feel good, especially if they want to keep them. It's worth pointing out that different genres allow varying standards of physical quality: for example, mass market fiction, designed to disintegrate on the beach, may be cheaper than literary fiction, and that is not a problem. Next, read the text on the back: is it well-written? (A crappy blurb is a dead giveaway for unprofessionalism and I find it astonishing that anyone would not spend a great deal of time honing a blurb to perfection.)

Don't judge a publisher by its size: big and small both have advantages and disadvantages. Judge by its books and where they are found. Many perfectly successful books are not found in physical bookshops but in book-club catalogues or online, but the point is that they should be available without enormous difficulty, otherwise it looks as though the publisher has distribution problems. A question to ask nowadays is whether they are properly exploiting the possibilities of ebooks, since this is a very sensible and important route to be taking. If books are readily available neither in print nor in ebook version, I'd worry. Ideally, they should be available

---

25 A term coined by James D MacDonald.

in both, though most publishers have not put their backlist[26] into electronic formats.

AGENT OR PUBLISHER: DIFFERENCES IN SUBMISSION

In most ways, your submission will be very similar whether to agent or publisher. There are, however, a few small differences, which all stem from one main one: your agent is interested in your career, whereas a publisher is interested in this book, and possibly the next couple if you are lucky. So, the agent is you-focused and the publisher is book-focused.

Some resulting differences:

* Your covering letter should reflect this. While both treat the book as central, the one to the agent will be more personal, conveying a greater sense of who you are, whereas the letter to the publisher would focus more on the book and its potential.

* Every approach you make, even to two agents, must be slightly different anyway, because every submission should be individually tailored.

* Since many agents are independent, working alone or in a small partnership, they are often overwhelmed by submissions. Also, they will be unlikely to have interns or juniors to filter submissions for them. You need to be

---

26 Backlist refers to previously published books. Frontlist refers to new books being currently promoted.

sensitive to this and not demand too much time or too prompt a reply.

✳ For the same reason, agents often don't like it when a writer approaches several at once – known as multiple submissions. I talk about how to deal with this in **Multiple Simultaneous Submissions.**

You will save a great deal of heartache by understanding the position of both publishers and agents when you approach each. The more you can see the world through the eyes of the person who will read your book at every stage, the more likely you are to get it right.

DO YOU NEED CONTACTS?

As in influential people, not lenses. No. Although you might be able to open some doors and have your work read sooner, this will not alter the fact that your book has to be good enough. So, if your book is any good, knowing someone in the business can speed things along. But if it isn't up to scratch, having contacts won't open doors.

However, the more knowledgeable people you know, the more you will learn things that might make you a better writer or help you behave in a more constructive way. Knowing people, making contacts and being personable are all useful aspects of getting along as humans, social creatures that we are. Nowadays, there are opportunities for everyone to become connected to influential people – with blogging,

Twitter, conferences, groups of every description. There are few excuses for not being in touch with writers and others who will offer advice. So, get connected, not because someone might publish you on the basis of your Twitter style, but because you will learn more about the business.

I didn't know anyone when I was trying to become published, but then I was trying to get published in the days before all this easy connectivity. Now, the world is your oysterbed. Get out there and gather pearls.

SUBMITTING YOUR WORK

Before we come to standard practice, there are some nitty gritty things that aspiring writers have trouble with.

EACH APPROACH MUST BE INDIVIDUAL

Do not use "form submissions"[27] or agencies to do this for you. Only self-publishing or vanity presses respond well to such approaches. (They respond well to everything, because they want your business.) Good agents and publishers hate form submissions because using them shows that you are lazy and because form submissions fail to acknowledge that each publisher or agent is different. Your submission to agent A may vary only slightly from that to agent B, if agents A and B are similar; but if agent A suspects that you've not thought

---

27   A submission letter which is the same for every recipient, with, at most, only the name changed.

about this submission distinctly, she will be mightily miffed. You do not want an agent to be mightily miffed when she reads your work. Really.

Many agents and publishers have written down their preferences for submissions. If they have taken the trouble to specify, follow their wishes. In the absence of individual information, follow the generic advice I'm about to give you.

MULTIPLE SIMULTANEOUS SUBMISSIONS

Since publishers and agents often take a long time to reply, it's only right that you should be free to submit to several at once. Generally, publishers accept that you are likely to do so. As for agents: when submitting to larger agencies, multiple submissions are accepted practice – though still require honesty and consideration – but if you are submitting to an independent or smaller agent you need to understand a few things and behave carefully. An independent agent will not take kindly to spending a great deal of unpaid time considering your work, only to discover later that you'd been submitting to others without saying so.

It's not difficult to tread a tactful and tactical line:

* If the agent or publisher has submission guidelines, follow them. If these say you should not submit to anyone else simultaneously, don't.

* In that case, it is perfectly acceptable for you to say that you would like to submit elsewhere fairly soon but that a quick interim note of possible interest from the agent would allow you to delay this. In this case, you should expect to hear the very briefest reply within four weeks,

even if the reply merely says that the agent would like more time to consider it fully, asking for a certain period of exclusivity. If your intimation that you'd like to send it out soon brings no reply, then it would be acceptable to send it elsewhere after four weeks. This is a relationship between two humans and you are entitled to be treated decently. Simply be open and honest and understand the agent's position.

* If an agent or publisher asks for more time and requests exclusivity for a period, do not be tempted to break this. If it is already with someone else, you will need to tell the requesting agency that, otherwise you risk a very tangled situation if both end up wanting you. Do not try to be clever or play them off against each other. Be honest. Also, do not get your hopes up too much; yes, it's a good sign that they wanted more time, but a good sign is a very, very long way from an offer.

* If you do submit to agents or publishers simultaneously, say so. State that you are very keen to work with A but that you understand the competition out there so you have taken the liberty of approaching others. This gives each the opportunity to nip in and say, "This looks interesting – could you possibly give me some time before you accept a deal with someone else?"

* On the other hand, there's honesty and there's foolishness. You don't need to say how many others you've sent it to: "a small number" is fine.

* Actually, any more than a small number at a time is silly. What if you send it to twenty and they all reject it for the

same reason, a reason that you could have sorted? You'd be kicking yourself. Whereas if you sent it to three and this happened, there are seventeen out there who won't know that you ever committed whatever fault it was.

OBEY SUBMISSION GUIDELINES

I am always being asked things like, "Should I email my submission or post it?" "Phone first?" "Send 5,000 words or 10,000?" "What if my chapters are really long – should I still send three?" Writers get very tangled up in these details.

Usually, the answer is simple and two-fold: first, find that agent or publisher's submission guidelines and follow them. Follow them closely, unless you really think that although they said they wanted the submission emailed, they really wanted it delivered on a white horse at dawn, with a trombone serenade and three bags of Werther's Originals.

Second, where submission guidelines don't seem to guide you clearly or don't fit your situation, apply common sense. For example, if your book is not divided by standard chapters but sections with breaks, and the submission guidelines say "send three chapters", send an amount which corresponds – usually around fifty pages of double-spaced A4. And say in your covering letter that this is what you've done. If your book is a children's picture book, which will be much less than fifty pages, send the whole thing.

To give you a sense of how different the submission guidelines can be, take a look at the guidelines for these agencies:

The Greenhouse Literary Agency – greenhouseliterary.com
Fraser Ross Associates – fraserross.co.uk
Jenny Brown Associates – jennybrownassociates.com
Blake Friedmann – blakefriedmann.co.uk

Guidelines can change from time to time, so make sure you are following up-to-date instructions. Sometimes, a publisher or agent says he's not taking submissions, but that might change a few months later.

If an agent has no submission guidelines, you have two choices. You could phone or email and ask how the agent prefers to receive submissions and what she likes the submission to contain. (Don't ask more detailed questions – you can find standard answers in the following pages of this book and you'll seriously annoy her by asking what font she likes.) The reply might be, "I'm not taking new submissions just now so please don't send anything." Well, in that case you just saved yourself some wasted effort.

Your other choice in the case of a lack of guidelines is to use your intuition and common sense. I'm a great fan of these two attributes and, frankly, they are all too rare in this business. Add them to the advice which follows in these pages, and you'll be fine.

While on the subject of common sense, do not ever – I mean ever – nag or pitch to an agent or publisher on Twitter or in the ladies at a conference.

WHAT ABOUT TRYING TO BE DIFFERENT? STANDING OUT FROM THE CROWD?

I know: it's tempting. I like being different myself. Also, you'll occasionally hear an agent say she loved so-and-so's approach because it made her laugh. So, you can risk this if you want to but it *is* a risk and reduces your chances of success. Thing is, unless you know the publisher's sense of humour and mood, you may get it horribly wrong. One writer's idea of zany can be a publisher's idea of lunatic. And, although some publishers may enjoy zany, all of them want a good book. So, if zany happens to nab you a deal, it was because your book was great, not because you were zany.

If you want to take the off-the-wall approach, I urge you first to read this whole section, because there are some things you really must avoid. There's off-the-wall and there's stupid.

THE BRICK WALL: "NO UNSOLICITED SUBMISSIONS"

Often, a publisher's website says it does not accept unsolicited submissions. This means they only want to see things that come through an agent. And you don't have an agent, so does this mean you can't submit? Not necessarily. The key is in the word "unsolicited" and in the reason behind the instruction. The reason publishers say this is simple: they want to publish wonderful books, but they have decided that the most likely way to find one is not to wade through acres of bog, but wait for agents to deliver it to their lap, mud-free. They have noticed that agents provide a wonderful service of slush reduction.

And the key in the word "unsolicited"? The point is that if you contact a publisher, not by sending your material but by pitching your fabulous idea and your marvellous self in a small handful of perfect sentences, and if this is indeed something they like the sound of, the publisher might ask you to send your submission. This is then not unsolicited. Problem solved and without having to disobey an instruction. You then send your sample, synopsis and covering letter (or non-fiction proposal) in the normal way, prefacing your letter with something to remind them that they said you could. If, however, your handful of honed sentences gets you nowhere, don't be annoyed. They don't have to read what they didn't ask for.

HIDE YOUR INNER GRAPHIC DESIGNER

Please don't go all snazzy with fonts. Snazzy fonts are for kids. You're a serious grown-up and even if you've written something of glorious wackiness, an ordinary clear font is what you should give it. Same applies to every part of your submission. Especially eschew Comic Sans. Publishers have a real thing about it. I think it's quite cute myself, but then I used to teach kids to read. Maybe that's the point about Comic Sans.

Obviously, if you *are* a graphic designer and your book genuinely requires design elements which you feel won't wait for the publisher's design team, go for it, preferably just by roughing out a few pages rather than doing the whole MS. But otherwise, leave it to the professionals. You will not jeopardise your chances at all by simply presenting clear text.

SMALL BUT IMPORTANT POINTS FOR ALL

∗ If you want a manuscript back, you must include a sufficiently large self-addressed envelope and the right postage. However, if someone has actually read it, it may well come back stained by blood, sweat and tears. Rarely does it come back in a state you can re-send, unless it hasn't been read. Please bear this in mind if you are sending any sort of illustration: never send something you will be sad to see wrecked.

∗ Focus on clarity, cleanness, common sense and professionalism, from the words you write to the paper you use. Make it as easy and comfortable to read as possible.

HOW PERFECT IS PERFECT?

There are three sorts of submissions.

1. The premature submission. It is very far from perfect but the writer doesn't know or doesn't care. This writer is either talentless, lazy, too impatient, or not prepared to countenance the idea that the book might not be good enough.

2. The OCD submission. This is rarely actually submitted, because the writer can't bring himself to declare it ready for public viewing. This writer is paralysed by self doubt.

3. The Goldilocks submission. Neither too imperfect

nor too perfect, just as perfect as you can get it without having a nervous breakdown.

There is no such thing as A Perfect Submission. There is only *your* perfect submission, the best way to show off your lovely book. So, just make sure that you've done your best to follow all the advice on these pages, and that you've committed none of the heinous sins mentioned, and that's perfect to me.

STANDARD SUBMISSION PACKAGE – FICTION

NOTE: A fiction submission must be for a novel which you have completed. Gone are the days when you could expect to sell it after writing four brilliant chapters.

THE NORMAL UK SUBMISSION

This is somewhat different from a US "query", though that is creeping UK-wards. Both models have the same aim: to show most clearly and easily what you've got. If you are submitting in the UK, and if you are confident about the needs of UK publishers, there's no problem with incorporating aspects of the US model if this seems right for your book and for that publisher. But always remember: following the agent or publisher's guidelines is your paramount aim where possible. I'll show you how the US query works a little later.

A normal UK fiction submission consists of three basic

items: covering letter, synopsis and sample chapters. It should be emailed or posted, depending on the recipient's preference. If the preference is not in the guidelines, I suggest you email it and add that you're happy to post it if they prefer.

Some people might advise you to email or phone to ask whether to email or post your submission. You could do that, but there is a risk that you'll be told they are not accepting submissions, even if the website did not say so. I would probably take that risk, because I wouldn't want to waste my time submitting to a company which didn't want submissions. On the other hand, you lose little by emailing your submission without asking.

Although emails can overwhelm agents and editors and can be easily ignored, they are also easy to answer. They are free for both sender and recipient and are environmentally friendly.

Besides, if people don't say what they prefer, they can't blame you for getting it wrong, can they? (It's also worth saying that the move towards electronic only is so fast that by the time you read this, the idea of posting something may be absurd. I apologise.)

Two disadvantages of emails are that they are easily deleted and that most people find it harder to read a large document on a computer. However, agents and editors now often put documents onto e-readers, which almost replicate the experience of paper reading. So, on balance and if in doubt, I would email my submission. That's what agents do when sending manuscripts to publishers, after all.

THE COVERING LETTER

This should take you a ridiculously long time to write because you must make it very brilliant. "What?" I hear you say. "Isn't it the book that counts? You mean I could be rejected on the basis of the letter, even if the book is great?" Yes, it is the book that counts but a) the letter can very easily hide your book's greatness and b) the agent may not get as far as your book. Besides, if you can write a book, why can't you write a letter?

General points about covering letters

* Follow the traditional rules of writing letters, including layout, date and signing off. If in doubt, err on the side of formality. Don't say, "Hi, hot-shot agent."

* It's fine to use single line-spacing for the letter, but do ensure adequate margins.

* Include full contact details.

* Be truthful.

* Be respectful but not sycophantic. Show that you know who this agent/publisher is and what they do.

* Be professional. Don't make derogatory remarks about publishing, readers, or your competitors.

* Be grammatically perfect – but not pompously so. Rather than labour a perfectly correct but turgid structure, re-word to create something more stylish.

* Be brief. There is no rule about how brief but if you can fit it on one side of A4, with good spacing top and bottom, this is good. Brevity is definitely a virtue – because it is a writing skill and because it will help the recipient. But not if you leave out really important facts.

Essential elements

* First paragraph: genre, age range if not for adults, and final length (to nearest 1000 words).

* Second paragraph (and possibly third, if necessary): a brief but perfect and powerful description of your book, focusing on the hook. This is called the pitch and its aim is to snare your reader. You must encapsulate the book's core conflict and main character and why we should care. Be specific, not abstract; objective not opinion-based. Use your utmost skills to get it right: this is what the agent or editor needs to persuade the people who make the decision about buying your book. (I suggest you revisit my words about **Hooks** in Section Two of this book.)

* Next paragraph: give brief, relevant points about yourself and your experience. This aims to show (but not tell) the recipient that you are serious about writing and well-read in this genre, not a fly-by-night; mention whether you are published (and, if so, give brief and best examples and omit flimsy, unpaid, online items), and anything which portrays you as a good prospect. If you have a platform through blogging or a speaking career, now is the time to mention it, but only if it is genuinely a good platform, not just because you have a blog with a few dozen readers and your mother. This is also the place to mention, very

briefly, any other books you are planning – if they are relevant, but probably not if they are in a different genre. Don't over-egg any flimsy points: better to be unpublished than to have a single online story to your name. You are trying briefly to show commitment and serious focus, not tell your life-story or scrape the barrel.

* A simple paragraph to round off. This would mention whether you're sending it to other agents and finish with something that will make the reader see you as a wonderfully professional and clued-up writer.

Things your covering letter must not include

* Typos or crossings out. If you make a mistake and don't notice till after printing it, reprint it.

* Sycophancy or creepy compliments.

* Boasting or value statements such as "exciting" or "brilliant". Objective descriptions such as "fast-moving" are fine. Your brilliance should be clear from your writing, not from your judgments.

* Claims that anyone in your family, circle of friends or acquaintances has read and loved it. Or school pupils. Or anyone, actually, unless of serious and relevant status in the writing world. (Though see my third point under **Things to think carefully about**, below.) When I say "relevant", I mean, for example, that a comment from a top historian carries no weight in the pitch for a children's book.

* Comments about how much you love writing and how long you've been writing for – unless you can back that up with serious publication history. Your love for writing should be a given.

* An instruction for the recipient to go and look at your website or blog. Of course the address should be on your letterhead or signature – unless your blog is purely personal, irrelevant or embarrassing – but they should not have to bother to visit it in order to understand what sort of book you're sending them. If they wish to, they will, without your bossing them about.

* A tacky email address – for example, dizzzeegurl@lol.com. Or one borrowed from your husband – such as Richard@hunkymuscleman.com when your name is Sarah.

* "Wee extras" – such as toffee or a photo of you dressed as a koala (or even not dressed as a koala). Publishers will send stupid stuff to reviewers when they send your book out for review, but they get sneery when you try to do the same to them. So, cut the gimmicks.

* Smileys, LOLs, ROTFLs. Geddit?

* Exclamation marks unless grammatically required.

* CAPITAL LETTERS FOR EMPHASIS. But your book title can be in capitals.

* "I know you're going to love this." Or anything that tells the recipient what to think.

* "My book has cross-over potential." Not for you to say.

* "My book has film potential." Yeah, don't they all?

* The phrase "fiction novel" – what is a non-fiction novel?

* Moronic comparisons: "My book is a kind of **Clockwork Orange** meets **Bridget Jones's Diary**". Or "the style of Jane Austen with the power of George Orwell."

Things to think carefully about

Some things *can* work but only if you wear your most sensible hat while considering whether and how to express them.

* Saying that your novel is based on personal experience. Sometimes this raises a red flag: it might suggest that you're obsessed with one topic, which is fine if it's a genuinely commercial topic. But the agent may doubt whether you'll write a second book. However, it may be that you've worked in horse-racing or in the City of London for many years and have some thrillers set in the racing or financial world up your sleeve, as would apply to Dick Francis and Michael Ridpath. In that case, great. But don't come over as someone who is simply turning life into a novel. You'll have *hopeless naïf* written on your forehead. Avoid the phrase, "My qualification to write this novel…" because there are no qualifications to write novels, only the ability to write novels. A better expression might be something like this: "My career as a head groom and then trainer in stables across the UK, and my recent work for the Jockey Club, give me knowledge of the

extraordinary world of racing, a world rich in intrigue and potential for drama."

* Mentioning that you've been on a creative writing course – if it's a reputable one, this is fine, but if it's not, it's worse than not having been on one at all.

* Comparing your book to another – not impossible but tricky to get right. It's sometimes a tad arrogant-sounding and risks putting people off if they happen not to like the other book (and usually unnecessarily, since your book is probably not as much like the other book as you think.) Also, you don't want to sound derivative. But occasionally it can be helpful, done properly.

* Mentioning feedback you've received – feedback is only as good as the person who gave it and it must be true and verifiable. A comment from a literary consultancy carries very little weight, I'm afraid, because the agent knows that you've picked out the good comment and omitted the negatives; also, many consultancies have a bad name for over-egging their reports with praise. On the other hand, if a genuinely useful person has said something powerful and has given you permission to quote, fine. Just be careful to avoid sounding naïve. Far, far better to let the recipient judge everything for himself.

The best advice I can give, other than only to submit your work while sober, is to assume that the person who will receive it is in a really bad mood, has had a week of dire submissions, and has just been to the dentist. That was precisely my own agent's situation when she once received a submission containing toffees.

THE DREADED SYNOPSIS

Too much sweat is secreted over synopses. Yes, they are important and useful but there are different ways to get them right and the synopsis is unlikely to lose you a deal if the letter and sample are wonderful. (Unless the synopsis is terrible, of course.) A synopsis is there to help you and the agent or publisher. Treat it as your friend.

One trouble with synopses is that they reduce your beautiful words to something plainer. They are your glorious self undressed and made to stand in front of the cameras in a Victorian swimming-costume under bright lights with no make-up. Well, in that situation, you would make sure you looked as good as possible, wouldn't you? You wouldn't slouch there, letting your abdominal muscles slide earthwards – you'd hold them in, put your shoulders back, chin up. You'd try to show that *if* you had clothes and make-up and corsetry on, you'd look sensational. A synopsis, being your story undressed, needs to do this. It must stand with confidence, poise, structure and form. Use those muscles: they're there somewhere.

The other trouble with synopses is that not everyone has the same idea as to how much or what should be in one. So, in trying to work out what to include, you must find a sensible middle ground, and work out something which does your book justice in the clearest and most readable way possible. In giving the advice that follows, I have used the views of a great number of agents and editors, as well as published authors, and attempted to come up with a norm.

Perhaps it's best to start by saying what a synopsis is not: it is not an outline. An outline is a detailed ... er ... outline of everything that happens in your book, including sub-plots and minor characters. An outline's purpose is to ensure that the plot hangs together. It is something that you would most likely write for yourself, not for a prospective agent. An editor might like to see it at some point, but it's not what you put in your submission. I usually write an outline as I go along, because it helps me keep tabs on things.

A synopsis is much shorter; it shows perfectly what the book is like and what it's about, without detailed outlining. A synopsis omits sub-plots and minor characters. It specifies the main characters and their motivations, conveys the conflict, setting, theme, and denouement, and gives a sense of voice. The purpose is to give a clear idea as to how the book unfolds and how you have wrapped up themes and plot. While it will not usually be enough on its own to make or break a deal – unless it is utterly awful and demonstrates bad writing – it is useful and gives the publisher confidence that you have a book that works. A synopsis anchors your book. It frames it and nails it. Some agents and editors find them useful, while others don't: assume that yours will.

Writing an outline is boring because you have to put so much in. Writing a synopsis is painful because you have to leave so much out. Both usually fail to convey what you really want to tell the world – but they only fail because you are so close to your book that you want to put everything in. The trick is to be dispassionate in your struggle to decide what to omit.

TOP TIPS FOR YOUR SYNOPSIS

* Keep it brief. There is no single rule as to how brief. If you want a rule, here it is: keep within two sides of A4. Some people won't mind if it's a bit longer but shorter is generally better than longer. Single line-spacing is fine for synopses, whereas it's not for the actual MS.

* Don't worry if you repeat something from the covering letter: the synopsis might be used without the letter at some stage in the acquisitions process so it needs all relevant information to convey just what sort of book this is.

* Always use the third person, even if the story is written in first person.

* Use the present tense, even if the story is in the past tense.

* Even though your synopsis need not mirror the chronology of the book, you should make it clear if the chronology is different. You don't want the agent to be confused if your synopsis doesn't seem to mirror your sample.

* Say what happens in the end, showing how you've tied up the threads. (Not everyone agrees with this but if you happen to guess the personal preference of a particular agent wrongly, this will not lose you a deal.)

* Omit minor characters and details of sub-plots, though you might refer to them; include secondary characters if relevant, but not tertiary ones.

* Don't ask unanswered questions, such as, "Will Jeff save the world?"

* Make the writing tight: you are a writer and everything you write should be high quality.

Other than that, you can make your own decisions about your synopsis. Different books lend themselves to different formats of synopses. If your book has a complicated structure or non-linear form, you don't need special rules: simply find the best way to show what the book is like, what it's about, and how you have tied things together. Know your book, find its core, and show how that core works.

Now, stop fretting about your synopsis, because it's time to look at your sample chapters.

YOUR WRITING SAMPLE

As always, the submission guidelines of whichever publisher or agent you are approaching have precedence over any other advice on these pages, but in the absence of instructions, these are the normal rules.

* Your sample must always consist of the beginning of your book, never random chapters. If you don't feel the beginning shows your work at its best, work on it until it does.

* The general rule is to send the first three chapters but if your chapters are unusually long or short, aim for the first fifty pages – very roughly, not ending mid-chapter, and

fewer rather than more than fifty. If your first chapter is more than fifty pages, it shouldn't be.

* Your sample must be: printed not hand-written; black ink on white paper; double line-spaced; in a standard font, not a childish, flowery or silly one, and of a standard size. For example, Times New Roman at 12pt is perfectly adequate. Keep the normal amount of margin.

* Pages must be numbered and each one must have the title and your name on it.

* The covering sheet must contain the title, your name, word count of the full work, and your contact details – postal, email and telephone.

* There should be no crossings-out.

* It should be clean – if this has been read and returned by others, you do not want the agent to feel he is the last in a long line of people with sticky fingers.

And that's it. Simple!

DO YOU NEED A CV FOR A FICTION SUBMISSION?

For fiction, a CV is not necessary unless the specific submission guidelines ask for it. If you have a couple of relevant facts or publishing credits, better to list them briefly in your covering letter. However, if your CV is genuinely relevant, there is no harm in sending one. I do mean relevant: major publishing credits or substantial employment within the publishing industry, for example, because those things speak to your understanding of the business of being published. Often, unpublished writers think that something is more relevant than it is. By adding items that are trivial or unimpressive, you look naïve. If your employment really is relevant to your fiction, you can easily say so in the covering letter.

If you do include a publishing CV, when you list things you've had published, remember to give dates and publisher. If you've won awards or been shortlisted, say so. Be careful not to look as though you are scraping the barrel: for example, do not mention that you had a letter published in a magazine or that fifteen years ago you had a true story published in **Knitters' Delight**. (For the avoidance of doubt, as far as I know, **Knitters' Delight** does not exist. If it does, I apologise for seeming facetious. Or even for *being* facetious.)

THE US METHOD

I mentioned that there was an American way of doing things which was sailing UK-wards, and that you might choose to adapt it, *if* such an adaptation does not contravene the submission guidelines of your intended publisher or agent.

The US method goes something like this:

1. Writer contacts agent or publisher with a "query letter" – just the letter, no sample or anything. I will offer tips below.
2. If the recipient likes the query enough, he asks to see a "partial" – usually the first three chapters or up to fifty pages, as for the UK sample.
3. If he likes the partial enough, he asks to see the "full" – full MS.

This system, though difficult to get right because the query letter has to work so hard and without the support of sample chapters, makes sense because the content of this letter is pretty much all anyone will get to sell the book on to each next stage. While similar to a UK covering letter, a query must also contain these important aspects:

∗ A little more detail about the book itself – apply all your wordsmith skills to encapsulate the book, including the conflict, character, setting and style, conveying a sense of exactly what this book is like. Yes, you do this in the UK covering letter, too, but the US one might have three paragraphs about the book, instead of one or two.

∗ More detail about yourself – including your "platform"[28] and why you will be an excellent publishing proposition. US editors and agents are keener on existing platform for novelists than in the UK, though this is changing, with platform growing in importance here, too. Keep your ear to the ground for shifting fashions.

---

28   Any public profile you have, such as a successful blog or speaking career, which will help the publisher promote your book. I will talk more about this in Platforms and Profile.

The best way to help you know just how – and how not – to get a query right is to direct you to the Query Shark[29] blog. Frankly, UK writers should read it, too, as it really does show you what agents and publishers want. I admire the US system, though I am glad not to have to work in it…

A query letter, as with a covering letter, is simply a way to pitch your book. Every writer needs to be able to do this and, whether it's five paragraphs or three, it has the same function: to make the reader think, "Wow, I must read that."

STANDARD SUBMISSION PACKAGE – NON-FICTION

Many of the rules for fiction submissions apply to non-fiction, too. Particularly:

* Follow individual agency/publisher submission guidelines.

* Make your submission clean, well-spaced, in black ink, with no weird or cute font. Etc.

* Show your book in its best light.

* The sample should consist of the first pages, not random sections.

But there are some differences

---

29   queryshark.blogspot.com

First, there is no need to have finished a non-fiction book before you submit the proposal. This is because, although you must have a clear idea of the whole content of the book, this is a proposal, and the publisher may well like the idea but wish to organise the book differently.

Also, you are likely to be submitting direct to publishers, rather than agents. Therefore, the focus should be more on this book than on your future career, unless for any reason you feel that this is simply the beginning of a more extensive career or a series of books. To know this, you need to understand your specific market well, including what other books are already out there and where the gaps might be.

A non-fiction submission normally consists of the following:

* The covering letter – this briefly sells your book in much the same way as the fiction one, but also highlights your qualifications and reason for writing it. It should also mention your platform, because this is going to be important to the sales team.

* The proposal – a brief document which covers: the unique angle of this book; the market/gap; competing books and why yours is different; more about your platform and how you would use this to promote the book; a chapter outline. The more you show you have studied the competing market, the better. You can organise this proposal in whatever way you want but the focus must be on clarity, structure and professionalism.

* A CV – if your career has been very substantially relevant

to this book, a full CV is useful. If you feel that your qualifications would more usefully form a section of the proposal itself, do it like that, unless the guidelines of this publisher require a separate CV. Be sensible about what should be included. Your two-week holiday in Patagonia studying the lesser twisty-horned mountain goat is only relevant if your book is about Patagonian lesser twisty-horned mountain goats.

* The sample – the first thirty to fifty pages, ending in a suitable place. The point of this is simple: to show your style, voice, writing skill and the type of detail which this book covers. Without those three things, your proposal could be stunningly compelling but your book won't be taken.

One of the biggest mistakes that writers make when submitting a non-fiction proposal is to think that the subject or their approach to it is much more original or interesting than it is. Passionate about your pet subject, you are likely to assume that more people will want to read about it than is the case; and remember that they must actually *pay* to read about it. You must aim for immense objectivity and ruthless, dispassionate market awareness.

This applies to memoir-writing more, perhaps, than to anything else. It is heart-rending to have to tell an individual that her very difficult life experience is just not interesting enough to the public; or that it's an interesting story but terribly badly told; or even that it's an interesting story but told in a mediocre way. It must be a fascinating and unusual life story, beautifully told. Many people have had really interesting lives, but not interesting or different enough to be published. If, however, you can extract the really gripping or different bit and wrap it up in a truly individual or interesting way, that could make a story worth publishing.

THE RIGHT TIME?

You will remember that my simple theory of getting published included the rule that you must not only send your right book in the right way, but at the right time. By this I mean at the time when that publisher has a space for it on his list. Obviously, you have no way of knowing when that time is. The internet is a clever thing, but it cannot answer the question, "Which publisher is going to be looking for a history of combine harvesters in Estonia by the time I finish this book in November?"

This is where luck comes into it. However, you can increase your chances of attracting the magic dust fairy.

* Send your submission out quickly after rejection or revision, and submit to several places at once where possible – see **Multiple Simultaneous Submissions**. If it's not out there, it can't be accepted, can it?

* For a non-fiction submission, a US-style query is a good solution, because it means you can approach several publishers at once more easily and quickly. For non-fiction, timing is more crucial than for fiction, because balance on their list is something they think about very much, so the wider your target the better.

* Networking can help in some unpredictable ways, because you might hear of a publisher looking for particular types of work. Please don't become frantic about this, though: honing your book beats honing your contacts list. It's just that, if you can manage both…

* Avoid sending your MS out in December. Publishers tend to close their offices from Christmas Eve till after the New Year and December becomes a rush to get tasks completed. Your MS will not be top of the list of tasks. Children's publishers and agents will be gearing up for the Bologna Children's Fair around Easter and all publishers and agents may be involved in the Frankfurt Book fair in October, but you can't avoid every busy time, so don't worry too much: just be aware that a reply could take longer at certain times of the year.

  Other than that, timing is down to luck and perseverance. You can't know when a publisher has just accepted a similar, rival book or when they've just decided their list is full.

SERIOUSLY SHOCKING SUBMISSIONS

Agents and publishers sometimes share examples of terrible submission mistakes. These are based on errors I've seen:

* Description of the model of printer on which the typescript was printed.

* The writer saying that most readers are thick and wouldn't know a good book if it came up and bit them.

* Sentences that simply don't make sense, or not in this world.

* A curse, to be activated if the agent does not offer a contract. Threats to name and shame.

* Comments such as, "Hey! This is your lucky day! Together we can take the literary world by storm!!! LOL!!!! ;)))"

* Sending chapters 3, 17 and 19, because the writer "didn't have the others printed out."

* Pointing out that the writer once had piano lessons.

* Claiming that God is the writer's biggest supporter and is behind every word. (This is a common claim.)

* Claiming that the idea came to the writer in a dream while on holiday in Lyme Regis.

* Glitter, confetti, nude photos or toffees. And several instances of tea-bags.

I must confess, I did once send a covering letter in rhyme. Each line was in a different colour, which made it a) prettier and b) more stupid. I was entirely sober so there's not even an excuse and I am deeply ashamed. I didn't get a reply so I live in hope that it was lost in the post.

Having said all that, if I were an agent and a writer sent me champagne, I'd definitely read the letter. It wouldn't make me like the book any more, but the champagne would help me compose a nice rejection letter.

One final piece of advice: never submit your MS while in the throes of religious or other mania, or high on hallucinatory substances. This is especially true of emailed submissions: even a small glass of wine can be enough fatally to impede a writer's ability to be appropriate. It's far too easy to click Send.

What you must remember is that the slush pile is so awful that all you need to do to shine from it is write a great book and submit it with a degree of common sense.

ON REJECTION

Some incredibly annoying writers get a publishing deal at their first attempt. I hate them. But being published at the first attempt does not indicate a better writer. It may mean any of several things:

✳ Easier genre or market.

✳ Luck.

✳ Dodgy, non-selective publisher.

We've all heard the stories of books being rejected many times and then going on to achieve spectacular success. If you are struggling to be published yourself, you will doubtless hang on to those stories, hoping for similar recognition of your hidden brilliance. It's a good notion to cling to, but hanging on and simply submitting the book over and over again is not the complete answer to rejection. You need the right attitude, understanding, and strategies for improvement.

Since rejections are likely to be things which eventually you will tell your grandchildren about and wear with pride in a kind of Henry-V-before-Agincourt type of way, let me tell you about mine. There were the occasional ones that said lovely things but gave suggestions contradicting previous ones. For example, there was: "We feel it's too short" after "We feel it's too long" and "The plot is somewhat avant-garde" after "The plot is somewhat traditional". There were the "Not right for our list" ones. There was my favourite – though not at the time – which consisted of my covering letter with the word "NO!" scrawled across it in pencil and returned to me in an envelope without a stamp, even though I had included return postage. For some reason, I found the fact that it was written in pencil extra insulting. And there was the one which arrived back the day after I'd posted it, which defies the laws of both postage and Newtonian motion, so I can only assume that the postman was employed by the publisher and sent to destroy the slush pile before it occurred.

There are myriad reasons for rejection. Including:

* Not right for that publisher.

* Not right for the market.

* No obvious place for it in a bookshop – therefore too difficult to sell.

* Too small a market.

* Good idea badly written or bad idea well written.

* Not room on publisher's list.

* Competing book on publisher's list.

* Editor didn't fall in love with it.

* Editor loved it but couldn't persuade rest of team.

* You made a right fool of yourself in your submission.

* You've written a perfectly decent book perfectly decently, but Venus was in the ascendant and the magic fairy dust monitor was having a bad day.

The problem is that you will generally be given little hint as to the reason. This is one of the biggest gripes by unpublished writers: "Why the hell can't agents and publishers at least tell us something about what we're doing wrong?" Let's think about this sensibly. First, they are busy with the enormous slush-pile of staggering awfulness; it grows daily and they simply don't have time to give feedback on all of it. Second, they are busy with existing clients and authors, which is how they earn their incomes. Existing clients and authors are very demanding – we do try – so agents and publishers can't spend more than a small part of their time replying to you. And, finally, unpublished authors often react unpleasantly to negative opinions. I know agents who've been told to rot in hell after pointing out the flaws in a work. So, don't be vitriolic, at least in public. In private, stick pins in whatever you want, punch publisher-shaped pillows and pain-dance on their imaginary souls. It won't make any difference, except to give you strength to continue.

There's another gripe by rejected authors, a gripe I shared. I used to complain to friends that so-and-so "hadn't even read it", as if this was intolerably rude and stupid of them. I used to hide hairs or tiny specks of glue on page 297 and be deliciously aggrieved when I discovered that the person hadn't bothered to look at page 297. Thing is, the first 296 pages weren't good enough. So, trust me on this: if page 1 is good enough, they'll read page 2. If page 2 is good enough, they'll eagerly turn to page 3. Etcetera. It's not a difficult concept. It's our job to pull our readers with us, not their duty to read more than they feel like.

DECIPHERING REJECTION

One rejection does not a disaster make. Several rejections are no cause for despondency but at some point you must decide whether a re-write is called for, either a flick of the duster, a major spring-clean or an entire house move. Without feedback, it's hard to decide, though you should always assume that you can improve your work and make it your main task to discover how. Somehow.

FORM REJECTIONS

Most rejections are "form" rejections. These consist of something which you can tell has been pre-written, to be sent out to over 90% of writers with the simple addition of their name at the top and, sometimes, a hand-written "I wish you luck in placing your work elsewhere" at the bottom.

Over 90%? Mary Kole, associate agent at Andrea Brown Literary Agency, writing on her blog[30], said, "I'd say I give about 93% Form Rejections, 5% Personalized Rejections, and 2% Revision Rejections." That's quite normal in a busy agency and Mary receives around 10,000 submissions a year. If an agent is only getting one submission a month, he might be able to spare the time to give more detailed rejections, but don't count on it.

One form rejection calls for commiseratory chocolate, five minutes of wallowing and a dramatic crumpling to the floor. Then, pull yourself together and send it out again. After several such rejections – there's no rule about how many but I suggest four or five – you need a rethink: search your mind for any advice gleaned while you were waiting, or any doubts you've had since which suggest how to improve your work. Then, apply these changes to achieve a new version of perfection, and try again with a different publisher.

Further form rejections call for an even more dispassionate look at your work, after reading as much as you can about writing skills, followed by some revision. At this point, you might require expert feedback, as discussed earlier. I very much hope that this book will have shown you much of what

---

30   The post is here: http://kidlit.com/2010/09/20/resubmitting-a-revision/

might be wrong with your book but you may not have put your finger on how to apply it yet. Someone else may need to show you. If this is the case, that's nothing to be ashamed of: we're all imperfect at seeing our own imperfections. I don't know a writer who doesn't need someone to point out the hidden, or not so hidden, flaws. I certainly do.

"Our list is full" is another type of form rejection and often a red herring. Yes, the list is possibly full, but if your writing is good enough and it is the sort of book they'd have wanted if the list wasn't full, a publisher will not usually dismiss you so abruptly. If the list is full but your book is otherwise perfect for them, they will usually want to give encouragement.

No form rejection tells you much, only that you didn't persuade them to take your book. Your book could still be anywhere between eel vomit and gorgeous prose of a sort that this publisher simply doesn't want or hasn't got room for.

REJECTIONS WITH NEGATIVE FEEDBACK

Your rejection might give a very brief reason. Apply common sense and don't necessarily read too much into it: it rarely tells you anything that you should act on, unless you get the same message from more than one publisher. Of course, if the criticism makes sense to you and you strongly agree with it, I recommend you act on it.

If the letter says that this is not the sort of book they publish, you are a very silly person who hasn't done the requisite research. On the other hand, I confess to having made this mistake myself in the old days.

Do not get involved in any correspondence about a form

rejection or one with negative feedback. Do not argue or disagree. You will get nowhere. Actually, you will: you'll find yourself in the naughty corner because publishers and agents talk to each other.

REJECTIONS WITH POSITIVE FEEDBACK

Some rejections give you much-needed encouragement. For example, they could praise aspects of the story; they might even say you should send the publisher the next thing you write. Such rejections call for celebratory sparkly stuff. They are relatively rare and very encouraging. After you've finished the sparkly drink, work hard to understand the feedback and to decide what was not sufficiently brilliant about your book. Do some more reading, if necessary, or find expert help. Then, work, edit, read, research, think, work, edit, work, work, perfect, edit again, and then send it out.

If you wish, you may send a brief thank you message to the person who gave you the encouragement. If she expressed willingness to see your future work, promise to work your butt off (but don't say "butt") to send something better. But do not expect to engage in conversation. You are not her new best friend just because you wrote something that wasn't horrible.

PARTIAL REJECTION ASKING FOR CHANGES

If the letter says that they'd like to see it again if you were to re-write it, this is obviously very positive. Take it extremely seriously, but be sure that you understand and agree with the suggested changes before you do anything. If you don't, you won't be able to do it properly and if it's subsequently rejected you will feel let down and confused. However, don't pester people at this stage, since they have to deal with existing projects and the last thing you want to seem is needy or irritating. It's fine to send *one* briefish email to check that you understand what they're saying, but after that you should keep quiet until you've done the work, unless they say they're happy to correspond more often.

Finally, if you say you are going to deliver the revised MS by a certain time, do it. If you are struck down by disaster or illness, tell them in plenty of time. That's part of being professional.

One rejection letter of any sort is not enough to go on. Several in the same vein should tell you something. A hundred rejection letters of any sort should tell you a great deal. Essentially, behind all these rejection letters is one message: you got it wrong. Sometimes you were just unlucky. But most often, it's simple: your writing is not (yet?) right.

APPLIED PERSEVERANCE

Perseverance is not all it's cracked up to be. We're always being told how essential it is but it's entirely pointless if we don't apply common sense and other strategies. If you are getting it wrong, there is no point in *simply* persevering. You'll just get it wrong over and over again.

A small amount of blind perseverance is fine. It could just

be that you've picked the wrong publishers for reasons you couldn't have known. But more than a small amount is a waste of time. You need applied perseverance: apply everything you have learnt to your work and then persevere in sending it out. Keep trying to improve your work and approach. Be like a greedy magpie in your desire to acquire understanding. Then apply it to your work.

As long as you are sure you're doing everything right, perseverance is all it's cracked up to be.

WHAT TO DO WHILE WAITING FOR A RESPONSE

Dead easy: you're a writer, aren't you? So you should be writing. You should be throwing yourself into your next idea. Otherwise, you'll look like a one-book wannabe. And no agent or publisher wants a one-book wannabe. No *reader* wants a one-book wannabe.

I recently came across an aspiring writer who was desperate for advice on how to get her multi-rejected novel published, yet who, when I asked what she was working on while waiting for acceptance, flatly refused to contemplate ever writing another one. "But don't you long to write something else?" I asked. "Isn't writing what you want to do?" She looked at me, appalled. "But this is my book – this is the one that must be published," she said. She wasn't a writer: she was a dreamer, delusional, unprofessional, uncommitted, and she deserved to remain unpublished. She'd been rejected dozens of times and had no idea why. She'll probably self-publish and then she will discover that the publishers were right. A reader, if she ever has any, might even tell her why.

Be fickle – turn your back on your adored book and fall into bed with a new lover. When you do that, you learn several important things: that your first book may not be as good as you thought it was; that you can fall in love again; and that you're a real writer with a much greater chance of becoming published.

DECLARING THE DEATH OF YOUR BOOK

Each time your book was rejected, you had to resuscitate and inject new life into it, but after a while you will – and should – begin to ask yourself whether there is any point. It might be time to let it go. It's the equivalent of the Do Not Resuscitate instruction sometimes placed on a patient near death. When should you gently say good-bye to your book and lay it to rest before moving on to another project? At what point do you decide there's no possibility of life?

Here are some symptoms of terminal illness. No single symptom is enough, but a collection of them should tell you something.

* Your finished book has failed – and failed and failed and failed – to be accepted, and you have had no positive expert feedback. (Note that I said "expert".)

* Everyone who reads your book has a different explanation for what might be wrong. The reasons either don't make sense to you or you can't see how to act on them. Or you don't agree.

* You are wallowing in negativity, vitriol and spite. This is quite understandable but it doesn't usually happen until the point where subconsciously you have started to believe that your book is going nowhere, and it is possible that you are right. The thing is, the truth is painful to recognise and, if you are in pain, it may be truth that's causing it.

* You have re-written it so many times that you've lost sight of its core.

There is one ray of hope, however: it is possible for your book to go into a long-term coma, from which it may recover some years later, but usually only after you have written at least one – and usually three – other books which are better. This process of writing more books not only teaches you to write better; it also gives you distance from that painful first one and allows you to grow into a writer who can write that first story so much better.

Whatever, it is time to do that very difficult thing which most published writers at some point did, including me: lay it to rest and start another one. This can be a defining moment in your writing life. Don't get me wrong: it's tough, it hurts, and grown men cry. But you will not regret it, I promise. Extremely few published writers have no unpublished work in a drawer. And I don't know a published writer who really wishes that their unpublished work was out there for everyone to read. I'm glad mine wasn't.

We have to love our books with a passion but sometimes we have to leave them while we look ahead to the next one to love. Call yourself fickle, call yourself callous; it doesn't matter as long as you are writing. Being a writer is about striving to be better all the time and this happens with practice. Let me say it again: the decision to let go of your work and start another can be an extremely important and positive moment.

PLATFORMS AND PROFILE

A platform is anything which gives you one or both of two things: an existing group of people who know of you and who therefore might buy your book; and profile or recognised expertise in your subject area. In other words, a platform makes you different from someone only known to friends, family, neighbours and work colleagues. In the old days, either you were known only to those groups or you were famous. Nowadays, a platform gives you a position in the middle of that and will be very useful in promoting your book, which is why publishers like authors with platforms.

But do you absolutely need one and, if so, when? It is becoming increasingly important, more in some genres – especially non-fiction – than others. You'll hear people say that publishers won't take an author who hasn't got a platform. This is not true for fiction but it's becoming that way and is more so in the US. Having some kind of existing presence or popularity will certainly do you no harm and in some cases could interest a publisher, but only if your novel is already good enough. On the other hand, even if it's not essential for a novelist to have a platform before a publication deal, it's still rewarding and can be useful. It will do more good than harm but only if you do it in the right way and are comfortable with it. Don't do it just because you feel you should: that will show, and when it shows it is self-defeating.

For non-fiction, on the other hand, an author certainly needs an established reason for authority before publication and the platform is part of that. If you're an expert in your field nowadays, a publisher would wonder why you have not displayed your expertise at least by a website, blog or public-speaking programme.

A note of caution: think very carefully before you say anything online. Although I advocate honesty and being yourself, this must be within reason: your online presence will become part of your public persona as a writer and you cannot afford to say anything you'll regret. Publishers and agents can read it, too, and it is crucial that you do not rant about them, even in general terms. There are well-known cases of online ravings which have gone all over the internet, and you so do not want that to be you.

PLATFORMS FOR FICTION WRITERS

For a fiction writer, developing a platform is partly about making contacts. Some of these could become potential readers; others will have something to teach you, or be a sounding board; some will become friends. But aspects of your platform are more than that: a blog, for example, is a wonderful way to practise your writing, find different voices, express yourself. It's easy, free, creative and the response can be instant. It is an extension of you as a writer. From your potential publisher's viewpoint, it shows your human and professional side in one go. They can see something of what you'll be like to work with. It's your shop-window.

BUT. There are three buts.

First, it is unlikely for an editor or agent to be swayed to give you a book deal simply because of your blog, website or tweets, but it is quite easy to imagine them being put off if your online words show you as unpleasant, greedy, useless or weird. I often hear aspiring writers talk as though they think agents spend all their spare time trawling the web to find wonderful blogs so as to offer a deal. No, they don't. What they do, however, is pass on information about weird aspiring writers whose drunken, delusional rants have annoyed them.

Second, a blog requires commitment, focus and time. It is not easy to build up blog-readers and not only do you need to blog on average three times a week, but you also need to respond to comments and visit other people's blogs to comment there. So, if you can't commit to this, don't start. (One good solution is to group together and share blogging commitment. There are several groups which do this. **Strictly Writing**[31] and **The Awfully Big Blog Adventure**[32] are two good examples.) It is also easy for your blog to take up far

31   strictlywriting.blogspot.com

32   awfullybigblogadventure.blogspot.com

more time than you can really afford. Take this from one who knows.

Third, although I said it was a shop-window, I advise you not to post chapters online as you write them. You risk problems. For example, a publisher would not be buying "first rights" because technically you would have self-published. Also, you are likely to make many changes before final draft or publication. Once you have a contract, you will not be allowed to post extracts without permission, even though you have retained copyright. I see too many beginner writers who do themselves no favours at all by posting their unpolished stuff online, hoping to get a deal out of it. One problem is praise from all sorts of readers who don't know what they're talking about, leading to a false sense of achievement which will not move the writer towards publication. Of course, if writing is just a hobby and you have no intention of publication, this is fine – but that's not what you're doing, because **Write to be Published** is about writing to be published.

Of course, there are rare cases of genuinely good writers posting instalments of their work online and getting a publishing deal out of it. Jonathan Pinnock's **Mrs Darcy versus the Aliens**[33] is an example, but he's an author with a substantial track record of mainstream success in short-story-writing, including being shortlisted for the Bristol Short Story prize. So, do it if you really have something good enough to sell. Most work in progress is nowhere near it and ignominy is more likely.

Don't be panicked into creating this thing called platform

---

33   Published by Proxima Books, an imprint of Salt Publishing, 2011.

just because people say you must. I'm sick of hearing writers say that an agent or editor has told them they'd better get themselves onto Twitter, when the agent or editor hasn't a clue exactly how or to what effect. Publishers, in my experience, are not always good at this stuff either, mainly because they confuse social networking with commercial networking or selling books.

Choose what will work for you. Be open-minded and positive, because your platform can be enormously beneficial and fun, but do not feel you have to do everything. If Twitter doesn't tickle your fancy and blogging seems too time-consuming, there are other things you can do, and I offer some suggestions below. Don't hide, though – the option of being a recluse died with Salinger. We all have to put on our best smile to face our audience. Just be nice, be yourself (within limits), be open and generous, be bold and modest in equal measure, and people will warm to you. That's what networking involves. It's not yucky or tacky: it's just what humans do, and some find it easier than others.

How to create a fiction platform

It's not easy to create a fiction platform before you have a book deal but at least you can show a prospective publisher and agent that you are willing and capable of doing all the promotion stuff when the time comes.

Let me offer suggestions for creating the beginning of a platform.

* Blog – this can be a good way to start and you'll be able to promote your book on it later. However, any blog set up with the express intention of self-promotion is doomed

to fail and you must always give much more than take. You need to decide the style and focus of your blog, its Unique Selling Point. (Mine, for example, is the Crabbit Old Bat persona, the painful truth approach.) Blogging for fiction writers is about making friends, being yourself – or at least an edited version of yourself. You can connect to other blogs and make friends with other writers. Writers are generous and will help you, but you should never ask for anything. Never ask anyone to link to you, for example: they will do it if it's right for their blog. Your blog is your castle – invite people in and treat them decently; and behave decently when you visit their blogs.

* Use social networking tools such as Facebook – the emphasis on Facebook (FB) is the word "social". Yes, FB is a great way to share what you're up to, problems and successes, but you can't use it just to boast. It would be like arriving at a party and announcing your publishing deal before you've even asked others how they are. Rude. But FB is a good way to make contacts with other people in the same situation and also to come across the librarians and booksellers who will be so important to you when you are published. FB is not the best place to develop a platform for an unpublished writer, though. Once you are published, a separate FB author page, on which you put your book news, works well, but only when you have a book to put on it. Your personal FB page is – or should be – private[34] to those whose "friendship" you have accepted; your public author one is available to anyone, which is a good thing if it's about platform-building. Also, that public page becomes a place where you can announce

---

34   However, you should be aware that anything you put online, even in what you think is a private or semi-private forum, could be seen by anyone because it could be passed on.

your successes without fear of annoying anyone, because that's where people will go in order to find out about your successes.

* And Twitter, which shares many aspects of FB, but has some important differences. Anyone – literally anyone with access to the internet – might see what you say on Twitter (unless it's a private "direct message"). This is an advantage as long as you never say anything you'd be unhappy saying in public, because it is public. Twitter is louder, faster, more frenetic than FB. It's more impersonal, though many of us have forged genuine friendships. It's a vast source of book-related news if you follow the news-bringers, such as The Bookseller, Book2Book, and The Guardian. It's where I hang out: it's my office canteen, water-cooler, photo-copier, and Christmas party. It's directly benefited my work, bringing speaking engagements, new readers, ideas, and paid work. I once sold a sofa on Twitter! On the downside, people do sometimes get themselves into trouble with unguarded remarks, or accidental public messages instead of DMs. My advice is: don't tweet while drunk or angry.

* Have a website – a more static option than a blog, but a good shop window to advertise yourself and show what you do. You can pay a lot of money or you can do it yourself for little or nothing, using free software such as Wordpress. A bad website is worse than none at all, however. As a general rule, a simple, clear and tidy one is better than an all-singing, all-dancing one with flashing bits and too much going on. You must keep it up-to-date, too. You could have a blog and website combined; in fact, that's often better than two entirely separate places.

* Use factual aspects of your novel – can you provide some research and resources for people interested in this topic? If you've done lots of research, don't let it be wasted. Your novelist's blog could become a destination for non-fiction writers looking for resources, too. (However, it's hard to do a mixture of fact and fluffiness, so do work out what you want your blog to be like.)

* Hang out in the right places – make friends and contacts. But don't annoy people. If you meet me, say something nice about my shoes and I'll love you forever. (Or at least respect your networking skills.) But don't trap me. Go to book festivals and get chatting to people after the event, in the signing queue or whatever; it doesn't matter whether that person is a writer or an actuary on holiday: it's all about sharing the same interest for a few moments.

Social and writing media are changing all the time and my advice is to see what your friends in similar situations are doing. It's these people whose experiences, connections and resources could help you most, even though I disparaged their ability to give actual feedback on your book.

PLATFORMS FOR NON-FICTION WRITERS

As I mentioned, platform is crucial for non-fiction writers, not just because it will be useful to help promote your book but because it demonstrates expertise and interest in your topic. Anyone can blog or have a website, so if you don't, why not? If you are passionate about your subject, and you fancy yourself as a writer, there is no excuse not to be writing about it. So, do it now and don't submit your non-fiction book until you have built up a following on your blog or whatever, or at least filled it with all sorts of juicy information which future readers will come to and which will showcase your skills.

Many non-fiction writers write about a whole range of different subjects, especially if they write for children. You, as an aspiring writer, however, are likely to be pitching one book at a time, so I recommend you focus your blogging and other platform-building on that, keeping your blog controllable and specific. Of course, if for some particular reason you feel ready to create a resource or platform for a wider range, don't let me hold you back, but do be careful to keep some coherence there and don't spread yourself so thin that people can't work out who you are and what you do. If you want to work simultaneously in two areas, or for children and adults, you might wish to have two separate blogs, two separate platforms.

How to create a non-fiction platform:

* Start a blog in which you write about and provide resources for your topic. Do it in the voice you'll use for your book. In other words, if your book is serious, your blog needs to be; if your book is witty and ironic, ditto. Provide a wealth of links to other resources within your subject area. Become the destination for people interested in that topic. Encourage communication and comment.

* Or (or and) create a website. The advantage is that it's less time-consuming once it has been created; the disadvantages are that, because it's largely static, it's less likely that people will keep returning to it. Have the best

of both worlds by having a website with a blog linked to it – you can probably get away with less frequent blogging then.

* Join Twitter (or whatever everyone's doing by the time you are reading this) – you need to be connected to people in your topic area. Twitter is perhaps even more useful for non-fiction writers than for novelists, because you can find the people actually interested in what you write about. On Twitter, make sure you engage warmly with people and build up friendship rather than bombarding them with information. They want you to be a rich source of information but not a know-it-all. The better they like you, the more they will listen.

* Build a list of contacts. Be organised about this: keep lists of email addresses and business cards from other people; get your own business cards made. Think carefully about what image your card gives out. Generally, a simple text-based card, with nothing floral or fancy, is better. Avoid pictures of kittens and puppies unless you are only going to write about kittens or puppies.

* Try to gain public speaking credits. Offer to speak to local writers' groups or interest groups connected to your subject.

* Get to know your local public librarians. They may know of local interest groups or hear when someone's looking for a speaker or an expert. And they can be so useful once you're published, too.

* Make sure that the local BBC radio station has your

contact details and knows your areas of expertise; same with the local papers – offer to write something for them. Local radio stations are always looking for news stories. Be useful, willing and professional.

* Pitch articles to national magazines, newspapers, relevant specialist journals, websites, anything to get your name and speciality out there.

One word of warning for fiction and non-fiction writers: I know I mentioned building up a list of contacts, but please do not think about sending a regular – or even irregular – mail-shot or newsletter to them. There are a couple of authors who send me regular round-robin newsletters of their successes and news. I have no idea what they want me to do about this information. This is not networking; it is just irritating. It has one effect: it stops me wanting to read their books.

When you contact someone who is not a friend with your news, you are asking them to take time out of a busy day to read it. The first rule of good networking is: give more than you ask. The second is: do unto others as you would be done unto.

TO CUT A LONG BOOK SHORT

Writing is a journey. It's often painful, usually lonely, rarely easy. But there are many moments of pleasure, and you don't have to wait for publication to experience those moments. The best times are when we write something that we are proud of, when the words flow and form something beautiful, when they say exactly what we wanted them to say. And when someone else reads them and responds as we hoped. Even better is when someone responds unexpectedly, finding something we didn't mean to be there. That's when we really learn the power of language and the difficult and special thing that we are trying to do.

Remember this: a writer who is published or who got a faster deal is not inevitably a better writer than you, but simply a writer with a book a publisher wanted to sell. What you have to decide is whether you are more concerned with being published or with being a better writer. I believe that focusing on the second leads to *better* success in the first, but focusing on the first can lead to quicker success and has less to do with the second than many people think. Choose what is important to you and then go for it.

It could be a good idea to do both, but separately. In other words, to have two separate strands to your writing life: the stuff that pays the bills and keeps you published; and the stuff that feeds your soul and comes from your heart. I'd love it if there were no difference but that is usually not the case.

Soon, you can put this book away. Reward and strengthen yourself with whatever you deserve or need in order to write – cake, sparkly wine, coffee, whatever – and believe that the best way to publication is to write the right book in the right way and send it to the right publisher in the right way. And then there will be only one more thing you need to do, the final piece of the puzzle: hope for magic fairy dust to speed you along. Because, yes, there is luck in this business, without doubt. My aim has been to help you be in the right place to attract that luck.

END PIECES

HOW WAS IT FOR ME?

This book is a case of "Do as I say and not as I used to do." I failed, as you know, for many years. Twenty-one years of failure to have a novel published. Towards the end of that time, I did have some small things published, home learning books mostly – they did very well in terms of sales, and many are still in print, but it was not what I wanted. I wanted, desperately, to be published as a novelist. Failure made me ill and consumed me with jealousy. It's not a pretty story. It's also a personal story, because every story of a writer struggling and failing is personal. Everything is wrapped up in it: health, family, psyche, location, support, income, and more. So, here's my story[35].

Aged twenty, wondering what on earth a Cambridge degree

---

35   With thanks to Jane Smith, of How Publishing Really Works, for letting me tell it first on her blog.

in Classics and Philosophy was for, I decided that I wanted to be A Novelist. I knew I couldn't earn a living immediately – hollow laugh – so I needed a job. I went to London, where streets are paved with wondrousness, and got a job cooking for an advertising agency, and dinner parties for Belgravia ladies who wanted strawberries only in December and smoked salmon if it was twice as expensive as the stuff their neighbours had.

And I wrote. I started a novel and also wrote stories aimed at women's magazines, *none* of which got published, because they were completely wrong for their market. I had something published in Reader's Digest and was paid £150 for about 50 words, an enormous payment in the early 1980s. My photo was on page one. Fame and fortune, I thought. I was almost right about fame: on a bus, I saw a man reading it, looking back and forth between the picture and me. I grinned. He asked me to sign it. My first signing!

Meanwhile, I was writing The Novel, on a cheap type-writer, while working as an English teacher. Somehow, in holidays and evenings, the novel grew and was finished. I sent it off. And received it back. Often. Each time I "improved" it. Trouble is, sometimes they said it was too long, and sometimes too short, so I was confused. One praised the original plot and another criticised its traditional nature. There was no internet and little advice available. I knew no one in the business, no one who was published, no one who was even trying.

Every time it came back, I fell apart. To most people, I seemed fine. But inside I was devastated that I couldn't find the key to publication. I didn't know what I was doing wrong. I felt useless.

After three years as an English teacher, I decided to give myself a year of writing full-time, really going for it, because being a teacher was incredibly exhausting and time-consuming and I couldn't write enough. I also wasn't well. I had glandular fever, toxoplasmosis and a couple of knee operations. So, supported by my lovely husband, I gave in my notice for the end of that third year. A month before term ended, I discovered I was pregnant. So, I didn't get my year of full-time writing: I got a lovely daughter. But I was still sending off that bloody novel, still getting it thrown back. I'd revised it endlessly and didn't know what to do. So I did the right thing and started another one.

We moved to Edinburgh and soon had our second daughter. I was still writing. But my health wasn't good and I now believe that this was down to the gnawing pain of failure. I wanted publication so much and I was trying so hard. I felt I was good enough, so why wasn't it happening? It wasn't enough to be a mother, wife, cook and damn good house-person; I wanted more and I wanted it so much that it was making me ill. Postnatal depression was diagnosed, followed by an under-active thyroid, followed by Chronic Fatigue Syndrome or M.E. The thyroid was true, and I still take thyroxine, but the rest wasn't: it was Bruised Soul Syndrome. I was damaged where it matters. I was happy as a mother and wife, but I had a chasm where "myself" should be. The odd thing was that to everyone else I was Mrs Efficiency, Mrs High-Achiever, Mrs Get-Christmas-Sorted-in-October. Failure was inside.

Then, a dull government organisation offered me work, writing documents. I sailed out of that interview feeling fantastic. Energy flowed through me. I still remember that.

God, those documents were boring but they gave me my life back.

But I still wasn't really someone who could call herself a writer, not in public.

The school where I'd taught had lots of kids with dyslexia, and I'd become fascinated. So I did a diploma in teaching pupils with Specific Learning Difficulties. That sparked an interest in the brain – a huge strand of my writing and speaking now – and a chance to be an expert in dyslexia and then literacy in general. I won't bore you here with the literacy work I was doing, as it's only relevant to the extent that it led to my first book contracts. To cut the story short, I self-published (badly) some home-learning books, sold the first print run of a thousand, and sent a set to the educational wing of Egmont. By chance, they were about to commission a major home-learning series, called I Can Learn. They asked me to write the whole series, for a glorious fee and my first experience of a nightmare deadline: twelve books in three weeks. Although it was fee-based rather than royalty-based, there have been reprint payments and internet spin-offs so I have been treated well. Also, when I do talks to teenagers now, many of them recognise those books from their childhood.

Anyway, now I could call myself an author. I was published. I was earning. I was valued. My books were in shops. I was reasonably well.

But I wasn't A Novelist. My second novel was still coming back. I'd had near-misses: a fabulous letter from Collins; a story being short-listed for the Ian St James Awards; several times when the novel got as far as acquisitions meetings. But nearly being published is still failing.

I started a third novel. I was full of hope. Sent the first part to an agent, got a lovely reply asking for the rest. (More rules broken: don't send a novel out before it's finished, but you know that now.) Went back to it, but didn't finish it because by chance I read a new children's novel. I'd been writing for adults and had never thought of writing for kids. Why would I? I wanted to break boundaries with language, not be held back by simplicity. Oh, how wrong that analysis was! The book I read was **Skellig**, by David Almond, a beautiful writer with an extraordinary voice. He expresses deep ideas in language which is only simple because it is perfect, not because it's trying to avoid complexity. He is unselfconscious and his words are crystalline and generous where mine were convoluted and self-indulgent. This was what I wanted to do. I'd been so tangled in prose that I'd forgotten about story. And now I could do both. From reading that one book, I learnt everything that I'd been missing in my failed quest for publication: that writing is about the reader more than the writer.

So I began to write **Mondays Are Red**. When I'd written about a third of it I became impatient and broke that rule again: I sent it to an agent and two publishers before it was finished. The agent and one publisher wanted to see the rest. I explained to the agent that I hadn't finished but would do so *now*, and to the publisher that I had interest from an agent and would be in touch soon. I then wrote furiously and sent it off to the agent. The agent said that she loved it but that she was now ill and had decided she couldn't take anyone on. (Pause for a scream.) I told the publisher this and sent them the rest of the book. Meanwhile, the second publisher, Hodder, rejected it. (Hold that thought.)

The first editor was very excited but wanted changes. She also suggested that I got an agent. I contacted two agents that day, one by letter because she had no email address and one by email. I included in my covering letters some glowing quotes from the editor. The agent I'd contacted by post phoned the next day and said she wanted to take me on. Just like that. When I opened my emails, I found a reply from the agent I'd emailed, apologising for not contacting me immediately. *She* was interested. Help! I contacted the first agent, explained and said I needed to know if she definitely wanted to sign me. Yes, she said. So, remarkably, I turned an agent down.

My new agent and I worked on **Mondays are Red**, and got it to the state we wanted it; but the editor who'd been interested wanted one change too many and my agent advised that we go elsewhere. She didn't believe further changes were necessary.

Which publisher took **Mondays are Red**? Hodder, who had rejected it when I'd sent it on my own. Useful things, agents.

Mondays are Red was published in 2002 and I have been very lucky ever since, though it has not always been easy and I've had my knockbacks. Authors tend to hide those bad times and you should realise that beneath every apparently successful author's confident exterior are bruises and scars. But do I wish I hadn't had the years of failure, of not knowing whether I'd ever be published? No. They stop me taking anything for granted or thinking too highly of myself. They are crucial to who I am now; they are also why I understand what gets published and why some perfectly wonderful writing does not.

Now, I am wholly well. I put that down to having repaired my bruised soul. In the dark days, a clever medical person told me we need heartsong in our lives and that the key to health was finding my heartsong. When he said that, I knew what he meant and where I needed to find it. That's why I spend time blogging for talented, hard-working, non-delusional writers and why I'm writing this book: because if you have that same need for heartsong, I understand.

PUBLISHING DEAL – FORGET THE CLICHÉS

So, what is it like, that moment when you realise you are really going to be published? It's different for everyone, but let me tell you how it was for me. You think I was starry-eyed with excitement? Skipping around drinking sparkly stuff?

Sadly, no. The news came in stages, during several phone-calls over a few days, mostly as I stood in the car-park of Ninewells Hospital, Dundee, while my mother-in-law, Alison, was dying. Apart from my husband, Alison was the person who supported me most vigorously. She had railed against every rejection, bemoaned the blindness of publishers, and constantly praised my resilience. She was genuinely and enormously interested and she wanted to see a novel with my name on the cover almost as much as I did. If she'd lived, my publishers would never have needed a publicity department;

the sales reps would have had a ready-made, unpaid sales force in Scotland; every acquaintance of hers – and there were very many – would have been persuaded to buy copies.

Alison died about a day after we finally heard that **Mondays are Red** was sold. Although she was unconscious all that time, I like to think she heard, too. A day or so before, my father-in-law and I were talking at her bedside; she had shown no signs of awareness for a while, and I said something to him along the lines of, "You know, I think this book is really going to be published." And she said, with her eyes still shut but with a definite smile, "About time, too." It is the last thing I remember her saying.

So, despite ending my years of grim failure, news of publication for me was not marked by happiness. I was standing in a hospital car-park, with my new agent talking about possible film deals and definite publication dates and that it had been taken as a "highlight title", and how everyone had huge hopes for it, and I had to go in from the August sunshine and sit in a neurosurgical ward, watching Alison lose her life.

That is why the dedication in that first novel reads, "In memory of Alison, whose belief in me was everlasting."

I hope you all have an Alison to keep you going. She'd never read any of my attempted novels, because I didn't show them to anyone, but she believed in me anyway, because I believed in myself. In her opinion, anyone who kept trying as hard as I did deserved to succeed. She was wrong, of course: trying hard and long is not enough. We have to be good enough as writers and write the right book. But she couldn't judge me on whether I was good enough, only on whether I worked hard enough. For her continued belief in that I am so grateful. I wish she'd been around to see the end of the story.

There's something else she'd have done if she were alive now: remind me to acknowledge what I have done. We need to do that. You will all have had successes and improvements, made new contacts and potential readers, had feedback that has inspired or re-directed you, written something better than the last piece, formed new ideas, grown as writers and people. So, before you return to your writing, do remind yourself how far you have come, how much better you would like to be and that your improvement and success are in your hands more than anyone else's.

I wish you all the success you deserve.

RESOURCES FOR FURTHER READING

This list is by no means exhaustive. Nor do I believe you should read all of these, or even a tenth. In fact, there's a danger in reading too much *about* writing, instead of simply writing. I've included books and online materials. I haven't read most of the books, but if I haven't I've heard about them from people I trust. I have looked at all the blogs and websites, but online resources change so I make no promises. I also make no apologies for those I've left out. It simply would have been impossible to include everything. Go find.

US – indicates that the resource is mostly US oriented, but I would not include it if I didn't think it was useful to all writers.

YR – indicates that the resource focuses on writing for young readers, including teenagers.

GENERAL BOOKS AND MAGAZINES FOR WRITERS

From Pitch to Publication by Carole Blake
The New Writer – subscription magazine, also online at thenewwriter.com
The Writers' and Artists' Yearbook published by A&C Black
The W&A Yearbook Guide to Getting Published by Harry Bingham
The Writer's Essential Tackle Box by Lynn Price (US but with UK edition published by Snowbooks) (US)
Writers' Forum – subscription magazine, also online at writers-forum.com
Writers' Guide to Copyright and Law by Helen Shay
The Writer's Handbook – published by Macmillan
Writers' Market – published by David & Charles, covers UK & Ireland

BOOKS ON HOW TO WRITE: NON GENRE-SPECIFIC

Many of these are by US writers. The writing craft doesn't change as you cross an ocean so everything applies. It's the publishing process and markets that may differ.

The Art and Craft of Writing and Getting Published by Michael Seidman (US)
The Art of Fiction: Notes on Craft for Young Writers by John Gardner – despite the title, this is not necessarily for young writers at all, and delves deep

The Art of Fiction by David Lodge – more basic than Gardner's one

Becoming a Writer by Dorothea Brande – published in 1934, but still relevant because it's about writing habit and method (US)

Bird by Bird: Some Instructions on Writing and Life by Anne Lammot (US)

The Forest for the Trees: An Editor's Advice to Writers by Betsy Lerner – wide-ranging and thought-provoking (US)

Booklife by Jeff Vandermeer – guides us through emotional and practical aspects of being a writer; very readable and unexpectedly useful (US)

How Not To Write a Novel by Howard Mittelmark – basic (US)

Is There a Book in You? by Alison Baverstock – psychology and practice of writing

No Plot? No Problem by Chris Baty – all about NaNoWriMo, (National Novel Writing Month), but full of useful tips about writing processes (US)

On Writing: A Memoir of the Craft by Stephen King – much more than a memoir (US)

Plot and Structure by James Scott Bell – techniques and exercises in plotting (US)

Poetics by Aristotle – amazing what that guy knew about structure and meaning

Solutions for Writers: Practical Craft Techniques for Fiction & Non-Fiction by Sol Stein (US)

Your Writing Coach by Jurgen Woolf – very detailed (US)

Wannabe a Writer? and **Wannabe a Writer We've Heard Of?** by Jane Wenham Jones – as the titles suggest, light-hearted but with serious usefulness

Write Away: One Novelist's Approach to Fiction and the Writing Life by Elizabeth George – a personal view but practical, too, as with King's **On Writing** (US)

Writing a Novel by Nigel Watts – starts at the beginning
Writing Down the Bones by Natalie Goldberg – focusing on freeing the writing spirit

ONLINE: NON GENRE-SPECIFIC

RESOURCES FROM INDUSTRY PROFESSIONALS

Some are also writers, but all are primarily agents, editors or other professionals.

Absolute Write – absolutewrite.com – wide-ranging, very authoritative advice (US)
and the **Absolute Write Water Cooler – absolutewrite.com/forums** – forum for writers to discuss wide-ranging issues (US)
Book2Book – book2book.co.uk – for all the book-related news, brought to you daily
The Bookseller – thebookseller.com – the UK-based book-trade magazine, in print and online
Behlerblog – behlerblog.wordpress.com – Lynn Price, a publisher's view (US)
Bubblecow – bubblecow.co.uk – Gary and Caroline Smailes, editor and novelist team
Creative Penn – thecreativepenn.com – Joanna Penn, Australian writer with good advice for writers
Duotrope – duotrope.com – resources for all genres, incl poetry
The Forest for the Trees – betsylerner.wordpress.com – writer and editor, also has book of the blog (see book list above) (US)
Grammarphobia – grammarphobia.com – two language

experts with a clear, authoritative guide to what's right and wrong (US but only the spellings are non-UK)

How Publishing Really Works – howpublishingreallyworks.com – Jane Smith, editor with deep knowledge of industry

Kidlit – kidlit.com – Mary Kole, children's authors' agent, with sensible advice of interest to all (US and YR)

Litopia – litopia.com – online colony of writers, with forums and podcasts

Nathan Bransford – blog.nathanbransford.com – former agent with much advice (US)

Preditors and Editors – pred-ed.com – spilling the beans on bad publishers (US)

Pubrants – pubrants.blogspot.com – another agent has a rant, but gently

Query Shark – queryshark.blogspot.com – agent analyses and dissects queries (US)

Rachelle Gardner – cba-ramblings.blogspot.com – another agent with generous advice (US)

The State of Independents – stateofindependents.co.uk – a blog by independent booksellers

Victoria Mixon – victoriamixon.com – editor and writer with no-nonsense advice (US)

Vulpes Libris – vulpeslibris.wordpress.com – a collaboration of literary readers writing about books

Write for Your Life – writeforyourlife.net – writer Iain Broome, who also has **Websites for Writers – websitesforwriters.net**

Writer Beware – accrispin.blogspot.com – essential for avoiding scams (US)

UK AUTHORS WITH USEFUL BLOGS OR SITES FOR ASPIRING WRITERS

Some cross genres, in which case I mention the main one.

Teresa Ashby – teresaashby.blogspot.com – short stories
Anna Bowles – chocolatekeyboard.blogspot.com and **annabowles.co.uk** – YR
Amanda Craig – amandacraig.com – author, reviewer and commentator
Emma Darwin – emmadarwin.typepad.com /thisitchofwriting – literary fiction writer
Sarah Duncan – sarahduncansblog.blogspot.com – also creative writing teacher
Neil Gaiman – journal.neilgaiman.com – a cornucopia of interesting things
Vanessa Gebbie – morenewsfromvg.blogspot.com –short / flash literary fiction
Tania Hershman – titaniawrites.blogspot.com – short / flash literary fiction
Mary Hoffman – bookmavenmary.blogspot.com – general book stuff (YR writer)
Tess Niland Kimber – tesskimber.co.uk/Shortstory – short stories
Katherine Langrish – steelthistles.blogspot.com – focus on fantasy (YR writer)
Roz Morris – nailyournovel.wordpress.com – also writes other materials for writers
Nik Perring – nikperring.blogspot.com – short and flash literary fiction
Sally Quillers – sallyquilfordblog.co.uk – insight into trying to earn a living
Anne Rooney – stroppyauthor.blogspot.com – non-fiction and contract advice (YR writer)

Scattered Authors Society – awfullybigblogadventure. blogspot.com – YR authors blogging collaboratively, including me (YR)

Joel Stickley – writebadlywell.blogspot.com – amusing and insightful

Strictly Writing – strictlywriting.blogspot.com – collaborative, various fiction

Tom Vowler – oldenoughnovel.blogspot.com – literary fiction / short stories

Bridget Whelan – bridgetwhelan-writer.blogspot.com – also creative writing teacher

Sally Zigmond – theelephantinthewritingroom.blogspot. com – historical, and short story tutorials

GENRE-SPECIFIC RESOURCES

Whatever your genre, as part of your first step to find information, see if the writers you admire have blogs or websites. Many are generous with advice. Some of the writers' blogs mentioned above are genre-specific and I haven't duplicated by listing them below, except in exceptional circumstances.

CRIME, THRILLERS AND MYSTERIES

＊ **Books**

The Crime Writer's Guide to Police Practice and Procedure by Michael O'Byrne

Plotting and Writing Suspense Fiction by Patricia Highsmith

Writing Crime Fiction by HRF Keating
Writing Crime Fiction: Making Crime Pay by Janet
Laurence
Writing Mysteries ed. Sue Grafton

✳ **Online**

Crime Central – **crimereading.blogspot.com** – (YR and
others)
Crimespot – **crimespot.net**
CrimeSpace – **crimespace.ning.com**
Crimefest – **crimefest.com**
Mystery Writing is Murder – **mysterywritingismurder.
blogspot.com**
Noir Originals – **allanguthrie.co.uk** – Allan Guthrie, crime
writer and agent, with useful links
SinC Guppies – **sinc-guppies.org**
Theakston's Crime Festival in Harrogate – **harrogate-
festival.org.uk/crime/**

ROMANCE

✳ **Organisation**

Romantic Novelists' Association – **rna-uk.org** – has a New
Writers' Scheme

✳ **Books**

Loves Me, Loves Me Not – ed. Katie Fforde
12 Point Guide to Writing Romance by Kate Walker
**Love Writing: How to Make Money Writing Romantic or
Erotic Fiction** by Sue Moorcroft

✳ **Online**

A brief internet search will bring up a wealth of sites, groups and forums – take your pick but **romancedivas.com** is often recommended.

HISTORICAL FICTION

* **Online**

Georgian London – georgianlondon.com – writer Lucy Inglis
The Historical Novel Society – historicalnovelsociety. org – has many links. Also see its magazine, The Historical Novels Review, which "aims to review every new work of adult historical fiction released in the USA or the UK" as well as a selection of titles for children and teenagers. It also publishes Solander – **historicalnovelsociety.org/solander2. htm** – with interviews, articles, short fiction and comment
The Virtual Victorian – virtualvictorian.blogspot.com – writer Essie Fox

FANTASY, SCIENCE FICTION AND HORROR

* **Books**

How To Write Science Fiction and Fantasy by Orson Scott Card

* **Online**

Forums and blogs for and by fantasy and sci-fi writers abound. Note especially:

Jeffrey A. Carver – writesf.com – includes free online course for fantasy and sci-fi writers

Katherine Langrish – steelthistles.blogspot.com – for children's fantasy writing
Online writing workshop – sff.onlinewritingworkshop. com – for fantasy, sci-fi and horror

WRITING FOR YOUNGER READERS

✳ **Organisations**

The Scattered Authors Society – scatteredauthors.org – support network which includes many friendly writers at all stages of their career.
Society of Children's Book Writers & Illustrators, SCBWI **– scbwi.org** and the UK one **britishscbwi.jimdo.com**
The Society of Authors has a sub-group for children's writers and illustrators – **CWIG – societyofauthors.org**

✳ **Books**

Children's Writers' and Artists' Yearbook published by A&C Black
Writing for Children by Linda Strachan

✳ **Online**

See the blogs and resources above and look for the YR designation.
Especially see **write4kids.com** and its **Children's Book Insider** newsletter

SHORT STORIES

✳ Books

Short Circuit: A Guide to the Art of the Short Story ed. Vanessa Gebbie
How to Write and Sell Short Stories by Della Galton
Creating Short Fiction by Damon Knight – literary market
Online (See also the writers who blog section, and note **Duotrope, The New Writer** and **Writers' Forum**, already mentioned)
Biscuit Publishing – biscuitpublishing.com
The Short Review – theshortreview.blogspot.com
The Short Story – theshortstory.org.uk – incorporating the BBC National Short Story Award
Tindal Street – tindalstreet.co.uk/writers – publisher with writing tips
Womagwriter – womagwriter.blogspot.com – by a successful women's magazine writer

NON-FICTION WRITING

✳ Books

Get Known Before the Book Deal by Christina Katz and online at christinakatz.com/
Taking Reality by Surprise: Writing for Pleasure and Publication by Susan Sellers
Solutions for Writers: Practical Craft Techniques for Fiction and Non-fiction by Sol Stein

✳ Online

Mistakes Writers Make – mistakeswritersmake.blogspot. com

Freelance Zone – freelance-zone.com/blog – not so much for books as general freelance work, but if you're a non-fiction writer you will need this stuff

ACKNOWLEDGEMENTS

Sometimes books have such long lists of acknowledgements that one wonders if the author did anything at all. If this seems one such book, I assure you that I did work rather hard. However, I was helped by encouragement, suggestions or comments, whether on the blog or Twitter or by email, from many people, and I know I'll have forgotten some. So, with a deep breath, my enormous thanks to Jane Smith, Joanne Harris, Mark le Fanu, Mary Hoffman, Catherine Hughes, Vanessa Robertson, Becky Hearne, Anne Rooney, Adele Geras, Lindsey Fraser, Kathryn Ross, Sally Zigmond, Dan Holloway, Nik Perring, Gemma Noon, Emma Darwin, Katie Fforde, Aline Templeton, Tania Hershman, Vanessa Gebbie, Tom Vowler, Gillian Philip, Lucy Coats, Daniel Blythe, Carly Bennett, Clare Donaldson, Tom Franklin, Helen Hunt, Rebecca Brown, Suzanne Jones, Helen Kara, Janet O'Kane, Cassandra Marshall, Martin Page, Sophie Playle, Tess Niland Kimber, Sarah Callejo, Mike Jarman, Marshall Buckley, Cat Gunn, Catt Turner, Juliet Boyd, Anna Bowles, Victoria Janssen, Andrea Franco-Cook, Cally Taylor, Allan Guthrie, Julie P, Col Bury, Womagwriter, Queenie, Clothdragon, various Janes, Davids, Michaels and Karens, as well as a Fairyhedgehog and a Spider. And not forgetting Anonymous.

More thanks to Emma Barnes of Snowbooks, for being an extraordinary publisher and saying yes to everything (so far). And, finally, all my blog readers, without whose friendship the blog could never have grown into a book.

Notes

Notes

Notes

Notes